TAKE THE CHALLENGE!

Word Fasting

CHANGE YOUR MIND....
CHANGE YOUR WORDS....CHANGE YOUR LIFE.

TIFFANY KAMENI

Word Fasting
Copyright © 2013
Author Tiffany Buckner-Kameni
Email: info@anointedfire.com

Cover design: Anointed Fire™ Christian Publishing
Publisher: Anointed Fire™ Christian Publishing
Publisher's Website: www.afcpublish.com or
www.anointedfirepublishing.com

ISBN-10:
0-9897560-1-7
ISBN-13:
978-0-9897560-1-3

DEDICATION

TO MY FATHER IN HEAVEN

This book is dedicated to the one and the only GOD there is: JEHOVAH. Thank You for being the wonderful FATHER that You are. You are my everything and I adore You with everything in me. Since you gave me this book to write, it is only fitting that I dedicate it to You. You have been my greatest supporter; but more than that, You have taught me that this book and every book I write is not to glorify myself; it is to bless Your people. The lessons, the rebukes, the chastenings and all that You have given me are welcomed by me because I love being used by You, and I love being loved by You.

Acknowledgments

TO MY HUSBAND JEAN MAGLOIRE KAMENI

You have changed over the years to become a great man of GOD, and I have been blessed (and stressed *wink*) to watch the process. It has been and truly is an honor to see you constantly transitioning into the man that GOD has called you to be. Thank you for your continued love, support and most of all, your continued prayers. I love you more than words can show.

TO MY PARENTS GERARD & ALICE BUCKNER

Even though you are not together as a couple, the both of you have been a continuous stream of support for me. Thank you Mom for promoting every book I write. Most of all, thank you for being there for me throughout the course of my life. Thank you Dad for loving and guiding me. Your faith inspires me to want to go harder and harder for GOD, and it is a blessing to know that you are proud of the person I am today.

TO MY PASTOR & FIRST LADY/ UNCLE & AUNT (THOMAS PAUL & GWENDOLYN WILLIAMS)

Thank you again and again for letting GOD use you. Every person has a time in their lives that is frozen in their imaginations; a time that has changed them forevermore. My time was the day I walked into Agape Storge Christian Center. From that point on, my life has never been the same. My change took a long time, but it happened and GOD used you to promote that change in me, and in HIS people. I tell people now that the evidence that a Pastor is GOD-led is by the fruit he produces. When a change is witnessed in the congregation, you will always know that GOD entrusted the right man and woman to feed HIS sheep. If GOD could change me, as broken and messed up as I was, I know HE can change anyone who desires to be changed. Thank you once again for your love, support and guidance. I love you.

TO MY EDITOR IRIS L. JONES

Thank you for doing an awesome job editing this book, and all of the books that you have edited for me. You have been and continue to be a blessing, and I thank GOD for you. Thank you from the bottom of my heart!

TO YOU: THE READER

A true and heart-felt thank you for continuing to support the ministry GOD has given me. I have noticed that many of you are continued readers who have read many, if not all of my books. Thank you once again, and I pray that this book blesses your life without fail. All the same, I pray that GOD continues to bless and lead you throughout your life's journey. Be sure to ask the LORD for understanding as you read this book. GOD bless you and thank you once again.

Table of Contents

Introduction

Word Fasting isn't just geared at helping you to stop cursing for a period of time; this book teaches you how to stop cursing by breaking the habit of speaking word curses. The purpose of the fast is to break the stronghold or habit that has bound so many. The techniques in this book are non traditional, and if applied consistently, will produce positive results. Even though every individual's results may differ and I can make no guarantees, I believe that when used correctly, you will find that word fasting will produce positive results.

It does not matter where you are from, you have learned to speak a certain way. Not only do we have accents, but we have ways of speaking that give off clues as to where we are from (both naturally and spiritually). In addition, the way we speak bears witness to what's in our hearts and where we are going in life. You may be an English speaking citizen of the United States; nevertheless, you still speak a language that represents where your spiritual citizenship lies.

To be quite honest with you, most people curse habitually, but the words they use aren't what we consider to be traditional cursed words or profanity. We were taught that certain words were bad or cursed and our parents often forbade us to use those words, but we were not taught that normal everyday words could act as cursed words. These are the words that do us the most harm because we use them freely, without understanding that they are setting things loose in our lives that we often believe to be attacks from Satan. In truth, they are simply spoken words manifested because of our own doing.

How many times have you said that you were going to stop complaining, cursing or speaking evil, but have failed? How many times have you consciously rebuked something that went forward from your mouth? One of the first steps to getting free of cursing yourself and others is to become conscious of the fact that you are cursing!

In Word Fasting, we will explore the roots of cursing and learn how to change our language to be one of Heavenly origin. This isn't just a how-to-fast-with-words book; Word Fasting explores the depths of the human mind, and how our words affect our lives. You will get the understanding you need before you start the fast to increase the effectiveness of the fast. Prepare your mind for the changes that are about to occur in it, and be prepared for a whole new dimension of understanding. Powerful-information packed read that will shift your thinking to a whole new level and help you to embrace the inevitable change that's about to occur in your life!

The Word Fast Challenge

Word fasting is coming against the words you choose by committing yourself to a time frame of not using them. Why choose the word "fast?" The human brain can be complex. When someone tells us not to do or say something, it is hard for us to comprehend because we are being told to restrain from using our GOD-given will. Therefore, when we tell someone that they can't do something, it often makes them want to do it. But fasting is a GOD-given principle that teaches us to reject the body, all the while learning to depend on the LORD.

Biblical fasting is to commit to not eating at all or to commit to not eating a certain food for a pre-determined period of time. During this period, the person fasting would anoint his or her head with oil and wear sackcloth. Today, you won't find many people wearing sackcloth when they fast, but everything else is still done the same way for the most part.

Word fasting is using the same principle that was set forward in the Bible, but doing it with words. What we will be doing is committing ourselves to not using certain words for a specific time frame. The goal is to stop using these words wholly. During this fast, you can choose to simply fast the words or replace the words with words that are blessed. For example, people often use the word "damned." This is a cursed word in the traditional sense, and it is cursed in the spiritual sense because damned means to be condemned to hell. When you hear someone refer to their children as "damned," they have just spoken a word curse over their children. This may be a habit for them because they can't see the effects of the words they have spoken and their parents may have used those very same words on them. Nevertheless, not knowing does not change the definition of a word, and it does not change the effects of that word. Because of ignorance, a lot of believers often cause

14

many dark hours to manifest in their lives, and this is when you see people rebuking the enemy and going into warfare. In truth, what they should have been doing is repenting and canceling the words that they sent out, or better yet, they shouldn't have spoken those words in the first place.

In the word fast challenge, we will not only learn how words affect our lives, but we will also learn to replace the words that we have allowed into our hearts. In addition, we will learn how to speak the language of Heaven so that we can release the blessings of GOD into our lives and the lives of our loved ones.

Are you ready to take the challenge? There is no turning back from here because a commitment has to be made in order for this to work. Word fasting doesn't tire out the physical man, but it is a workout for the mind. Our lives will not change until our minds change; this is a guarantee. But to change the mind requires introducing it to new information and committing that information to memory.

When taking the challenge, it would be extra helpful if you could get your entire immediate family or those living in the same house with you involved. It is easy to default back to speaking the old way when you keep hearing the same things; nevertheless, if they won't commit to it, it's still doable. You just have to commit to staying in it until you learn to speak as a heavenly representative.

Why Take The Challenge

If you are tired of seeing the same results and you want to change your life, this challenge is perfect for you. People usually try to trick themselves into speaking right, but such techniques are often ineffective and border witchcraft. We can buy programs and do things to try and force our minds to act and react a certain way, but anything outside of the WORD of GOD is not a permanent solution. Think about a drug addict or an alcoholic. Even after an addict has been drug free or an alcoholic has been alcohol free for years, they are still considered to be addicts because medical science says that they will remain an addict for the rest of their lives. However, they can learn to become dormant addicts, not giving in to the disease. That's the world's way of describing it, but let's review the way that GOD has carved out for the believer. Addiction isn't a disease; addiction is brought on by a demonic spirit and if someone is not delivered from that spirit, they will continually seek ways to pacify it. Anytime an addict tries to stop taking drugs or stop drinking alcohol, should they relapse, they are often worse off than before. Why is that? Matthews 12:43-45 describes what is happening: *"When the unclean spirit is gone out of a man, he walketh through dry places, seeking rest, and findeth none. Then he saith, I will return into my house from whence I came out; and when he is come, he findeth it empty, swept, and garnished. Then goeth he, and taketh with himself seven other spirits more wicked than himself, and they enter in and dwell there: and the last state of that man is worse than the first. Even so shall it be also unto this wicked generation."*

Any way outside of the Word of GOD will produce temporary results. When that unclean spirit went out of that man, it went out because it wasn't being fed. Demons require a certain type of food to power up. When they are not given this food, they will attempt to find another habitation, but in finding none, the spirit will return to its previous host. The problem is that the host has learned how to come against that spirit by not feeding it, so that spirit decides to bring in seven more spirits more evil than itself.

So, when you decide to word fast, your challenge isn't just to stop speaking words that release curses; your challenge is to be delivered from the root of those words, be it demonic or generational, so that you can remain free. You want to see a change manifest in your life; right? Learning how to speak, when to speak and when to be silent, as well as learning the words to refrain from will produce that change. The ultimate goal is to change what is in your heart so that what flows from it will be words that yield blessed fruit and not vines that grow up and choke the life out of you.

Out of the abundance of the heart, the mouth speaks. This is the WORD of GOD. The word fast challenge is designed to remove the wrong things that have learned to call your heart home and to move in the righteous words that GOD has spoken.

Origin of Cursed Words

As you already know, most people refer to "cursed" words as "curse" words or "cuss" words. In referring to profane words in this manner, the speaker doesn't actually pay attention to the fact that certain words are considered cursed. Instead, the word "curse" or "cuss" has taken on a whole new meaning for many. People now see those words as words forbidden by modern society.

Do cursed words really exist, and how did they come about? Many words that we consider profanity today were just commonly used words in English history and Roman history; nevertheless, the act that the word was describing was considered to be taboo or something you should not mention in public. For example, sex was never to be discussed in public; therefore, any words that had sexual connotation were considered cursed words.

Cursed words were thought to desecrate what is considered holy, and were considered by some to be a form of blasphemy. Nowadays, profanity is shunned, but actual cursed words are openly spoken. This is done because most people don't know the difference between profanity and cursed words. Profanity is simply words that were once considered taboo. Of course, I won't mention those words here, because they have taken a dark spin over the years, but they aren't the same as cursed words.

A cursed word is anything that speaks evil of another person. For example, the word "damn" is considered a cursed word because it means to condemn a person to hell. All the same, the term "go to hell" is a cursed term because it speaks against GOD'S will for a person, and speaks to the nature of Satan's desire for mankind. *"The Lord is not slack concerning his promise, as some men count slackness; but is longsuffering to us-ward, **not willing that any should perish**, but that all should come to repentance"* (2 Peter 3:9).

Cursed words can also be terms used to speak harm over a person, place, time or thing. For example, someone may attempt to curse the day that another person was born. Of course, if that person has been born again (the one the word was spoken against), those words would have no power over them; therefore, that day would remain blessed, but the speaker would suffer the effects of the word he or she has spoken every day. Additionally, the day they attempted to curse would be exceptionally difficult for them because that day would yield to them the fruit of their lips.

The Bible mentions two word curses that can be spoken because they lead to eternal damnation. One of those words is "fool," but only when referring to another believer. *"But I say unto you, That whosoever is angry with his brother without a cause shall be in danger of the judgment: and whosoever shall say to his brother, Raca, shall be in danger of the council: but whosoever shall say, Thou fool, shall be in danger of hell fire" (Matthew 5:22).*

Why is it a sin to call a believer a fool? Because a
fool is someone who does not believe in GOD, or one
who lacks wisdom. If a person lacks wisdom, they
essentially lack the presence of GOD because
wisdom comes from GOD and wisdom comes with
GOD. All the same, to lack wisdom means that one
does not revere or fear the LORD. Psalms 111:10
states, *"The fear of the LORD is the beginning of
wisdom: a good understanding have all they that do
his commandments: his praise endureth for ever."* To
obtain wisdom, we must first fear GOD. To fear GOD,
we have to seek first the Kingdom of GOD and all its
righteousness. According to Matthew 6:33, by
seeking the Kingdom of GOD first and all of the
righteousness of the Kingdom, everything else will be
added to us. Therefore, to call a believer an
unbeliever is a curse because it is the same as telling
a person to "go to hell" when GOD has provided
CHRIST so that the person would not be damned to
hell. All the same, such a term makes light of the
Blood of JESUS, which was shed for our sins so that
we could be reconciled to the FATHER. This means
that the speaker is dishonoring the temple of the

24

HOLY SPIRIT because when we are born again, we are the temple of the HOLY SPIRIT. This puts us in danger of hell's fire, which brings us to the second curse the Bible speaks of.

"But he that shall blaspheme against the Holy Ghost hath never forgiveness, but is in danger of eternal damnation: Because they said, He hath an unclean spirit" (Mark 3:29-30). Merriam-Webster Dictionary Online defines blasphemy as:
a : the act of insulting or showing contempt or lack of reverence for God
b : the act of claiming the attributes of deity
c: irreverence toward something considered sacred or inviolable

But what does it mean to commit blasphemy against the HOLY SPIRIT? We'll let the Bible answer for itself. Paul wrote a letter to Timothy, who was pastoring the church in Ephesus. The tone of the letter is to warn against false doctrine. Two men had been guilty of erring from the faith. *"Holding faith, and a good conscience; which some having put away*

*concerning faith have made shipwreck: Of whom is
Hymenaeus and Alexander; whom I have delivered
unto Satan, that they may learn not to blaspheme"* (1
Timothy 1:19-20). The Bible only speaks about
Hymenaeus and Alexander once more, and the
second scripture will give us a better understanding of
the crime they committed. 2 Timothy 2:16-18 reads,
*"But shun profane and vain babblings: for they will
increase unto more ungodliness. And their word will
eat as doth a canker: of whom is Hymenaeus and
Philetus; <u>Who concerning the truth have erred, saying
that the resurrection is past already; and overthrow
the faith of some.</u>"*

Furthermore, when CHRIST warned about this
unforgivable crime, HE was answering the Pharisees
who accused HIM of doing HIS miracles through the
power of Beezelbub. Of course, Beezelbub is Satan.
CHRIST was performing miracles; however, by the
SPIRIT of GOD aka the HOLY SPIRIT. To refer to
GOD'S SPIRIT in such a way is blasphemy. Just as
Hymenaeus and Alexander were turning others from
the faith by stating that the resurrection of man had

already passed. They were basically stating that mankind had already been judged years, decades or centuries ago. They were simply denying that JESUS was and is LORD, and that some other CHRIST had come and done this work some time ago. This was considered blasphemy against the Son of GOD, which was and is forgivable. This is why Paul said he had delivered them over to Satan to learn not to blaspheme. This meant that there was hope for them; they were simply being taught a painful lesson.

The word "blasphemy" comes from the Greek word "blasphemia." Blasphemia was derived from two Greek words: "blapto" and "pheme." Blapto means to injure, harm or hinder. Pheme means to speak against. *"Then was brought unto him one possessed with a devil, blind, and dumb: and he healed him, insomuch that the blind and dumb both spake and saw. And all the people were amazed, and said, Is not this the son of David? But when the Pharisees heard it, they said, This fellow doth not cast out devils, but by Beelzebub the prince of the devils.*
And Jesus knew their thoughts, and said unto them,

Every kingdom divided against itself is brought to desolation; and every city or house divided against itself shall not stand: And if Satan cast out Satan, he is divided against himself; how shall then his kingdom stand? And if I by Beelzebub cast out devils, by whom do your children cast them out? therefore they shall be your judges. But if I cast out devils by the Spirit of God, then the kingdom of God is come unto you. Or else how can one enter into a strong man's house, and spoil his goods, except he first bind the strong man? and then he will spoil his house.

He that is not with me is against me; and he that gathereth not with me scattereth abroad.

Wherefore I say unto you, All manner of sin and blasphemy shall be forgiven unto men: but the blasphemy against the Holy Ghost shall not be forgiven unto men. And whosoever speaketh a word against the Son of man, it shall be forgiven him: but whosoever speaketh against the Holy Ghost, it shall not be forgiven him, neither in this world, neither in the world to come" (Matthew 12:22-32).

As you can see, the Pharisees envied CHRIST.

When they saw that the people were amazed at the miracles performed, they attempted to discredit HIM by discrediting the power in which HE'D come in the name of. Did they really believe HIS power was derived from Beezelbub? No. They were simply attempting to hinder the advancement of the gospel. When Hymenaeus and Alexander taught a different doctrine, they were attempting to hinder the work of the Apostles; therefore, to blaspheme against the HOLY SPIRIT is to speak against HIS power, and to hinder or attempt to hinder HIM from advancing by speaking against HIM. This would imply that the speaker has a motive in speaking against the works of GOD.

Now, back to speaking against a believer, or calling a believer a "fool." When we speak against a person, we can be forgiven. To refer to a believer as a fool is not just speaking a word against the person; it is speaking a word against the works of the HOLY SPIRIT. Ephesians 4:26-32 reads: *"Be ye angry, and sin not: let not the sun go down upon your wrath: Neither give place to the devil. Let him that stole steal* *no more: but rather let him labour, working with his hands the thing which is good, that he may have to give to him that needeth. Let no corrupt communication proceed out of your mouth, but that which is good to the use of edifying, that it may minister grace unto the hearers. **And grieve not the holy Spirit of God, whereby ye are sealed unto the day of redemption.** Let all bitterness, and wrath, and anger, and clamour, and evil speaking, be put away from you, with all malice: And be ye kind one to another, tenderhearted, forgiving one another, even as God for Christ's sake hath forgiven you."*

As believers, we are being warned not to give ourselves over to anger. These scriptures indicate that through anger, we sin with our mouths, but we are being warned not to grieve the HOLY SPIRIT of GOD. Remember, as believers, we often speak to and of believers. We can become angered by other believers, but we are warned to watch our speech in relation to them because they too are sealed by GOD.

Finally, it tells us that by HIS SPIRIT, we are sealed unto the day of redemption. Since we are sealed by

HIS SPIRIT and inhabited by HIS SPIRIT, we are now new creatures anointed by GOD. To be anointed means to be chosen by GOD. As a believer, you were chosen by GOD to walk with HIM. Don't believe this? Romans 11:1-6 reads, *"I say then, Hath God cast away his people? God forbid. For I also am an Israelite, of the seed of Abraham, of the tribe of Benjamin. God hath not cast away his people which he foreknew. Wot ye not what the scripture saith of Elias? how he maketh intercession to God against Israel, saying, Lord, they have killed thy prophets, and digged down thine altars; and I am left alone, and they seek my life. But what saith the answer of God unto him?* **_I have reserved to myself seven thousand men, who have not bowed the knee to the image of Baal._** *Even so then at this present time also there is a remnant according to the election of grace. And if by grace, then is it no more of works: otherwise grace is no more grace. But if it be of works, then is it no more grace: otherwise work is no more work."*

What's the verdict? To speak against a believer is a

forgivable sin, but to speak against the power of the HOLY GHOST in operation in that believer with the motive of prohibiting that person's ministry is blasphemy....not against the believer, but against GOD HIMSELF. To speak against the HOLY SPIRIT with intent to hinder HIM is blasphemy. Of course, this is often done out of envy and malice.

Cursed words are words that were sent out with evil intent. It's not always the words themselves, but the condition of the person's heart determines whether their words are cursed or blessed. For example, someone may say to another person that they are going to lose their house. Most of us would say that they were speaking a curse, and we'd rebuke their words immediately. But if this knowledge comes from GOD and is a prophecy, it is not a cursed word or cursed statement, because there was no wicked intent driving it. That's why GOD warns us in 1 John 4:1 this way: *"Beloved, believe not every spirit, but try the spirits whether they are of God: because many false prophets are gone out into the world."* You don't want to end up wrongly rebuking a true Prophet of

GOD; all the same, you don't want to end up receiving the words from a false prophet. To prevent this, we are commanded to try the spirits to see if they are of GOD.

Remember, there is a difference between a profane word and a cursed word. Profanities are taboo words that are largely unaccepted in modern civilization, but cursed words can be everyday words that we use with malicious intent. Either way, our hearts should not be filled with such words. Our hearts are like bowls and our tongues are like spoons. Our tongues will always dip into our hearts and carry to the forefront the content of our hearts to feed the person we are speaking to. A person doesn't necessarily have to use profanity to speak curses at you; howbeit, when you are a believer, no one can curse what GOD has blessed. Instead, you would have to walk out of the will of GOD in order to receive the plagues of unrighteousness. You would have to go back into the world to be "eligible" to receive the substance of cursed words. James 4:4 warns the believer this way: *"Ye adulterers and adulteresses, know ye not that the friendship of the world is enmity with God? Whosoever therefore will be a friend of the world is the enemy of God."*

The Power of Words

Let's get one thing straight; you're a liar. Before you rebuke that statement, please know that it is not mine. Romans 3:4 reads: "God forbid: yea, let God be true, but every man a liar; as it is written, that you might be justified in your sayings, and might overcome when you are judged." How can you be a liar when you consciously try to tell the truth? The answer is simple and yet complicated: You speak only what you know, but what you know is severely limited to what you have been taught. Human nature is to fill in the blanks when we don't know the answers, but to GOD, our facts are lies. A good example would be cancer. A doctor may diagnose a believer with cancer, but is his diagnosis true? No. Isaiah 53:5 says that we are healed; therefore, what the doctor is seeing is what has manifested in the body of that man. It is a fact that he may have cancer, but the already declared WORD is the Truth. To be delivered of the cancer, the man would have to repent of the root of the cancer and acknowledge that GOD'S WORD is Truth. Let's go a little deeper with this.

"In the beginning was the Word, and the Word was with God, and the Word was God" (John 1:1).

"And the Word was made flesh, and dwelt among us, (and we beheld his glory, the glory as of the only begotten of the Father,) full of grace and truth" (John 1:14).

"Who his own self bare our sins in his own body on the tree, that we, being dead to sins, should live unto righteousness: by whose stripes ye were healed. For ye were as sheep going astray; but are now returned unto the Shepherd and Bishop of your souls" (1 Peter 2:24-25).

"Jesus saith unto him, I am the way, the truth, and the life: no man cometh unto the Father, but by me" (John 14:6).

"That if thou shalt confess with thy mouth the Lord Jesus, and shalt believe in thine heart that God hath raised him from the dead, thou shalt be saved" (Romans 10:9).

"So shall my word be that goeth forth out of my mouth: it shall not return unto me void, but it shall accomplish that which I please, and it shall prosper in the thing whereto I sent it" (Isaiah 55:11).

What conclusion are we drawing here? JESUS CHRIST is the living WORD of GOD. In order for cancer to leave someone's body, CHRIST has to be allowed into the heart of the man. The heart of the man is his belief system. This is where faith or fear resides. When we have faith in GOD, we simply believe GOD; which means, we allow the Truth or the WORD of GOD to reside within our hearts and manifest the inheritance of GOD into our lives. The inheritance encompasses every blessing that GOD has reserved for the believer, including healing. Fear is believing what Satan has declared; therefore, when you believe Satan, you are in the same saying that you do not believe GOD. GOD said that every WORD that proceeds from HIS mouth will not return to HIM null or void, meaning it will accomplish that in which it was sent out to accomplish. What did CHRIST JESUS do? HE is the living WORD, and HE accomplished what HE was sent out to accomplish; therefore, to believe that you are healed through CHRIST JESUS is the same as opening up the door of your heart to HIM. In doing so, you will become what HE has already declared because HE bore your sins for you. This means sickness and disease have no rights to your mind, spirit or soul. Nevertheless, if the doctor gave you a different report, and you believe what the doctor said, you are in the same believing what Satan has said, and it becomes a fact for you.

A fact and the truth are different. A fact is a statement that resides in the earth realm and has been proven through man's findings and man's limited intelligence. A fact is subject to change because it is man's version of the truth, and it only takes another man to conduct a study and disprove it. The Truth; however, is the WORD of GOD, and HE shall not return to the LORD void because HE changes not.

We have become accustomed to speaking lies on a minute-to-minute basis. For example, a friend may jokingly call another friend "crazy" when GOD said,

*"For God hath not given us the spirit of fear; but of power, and of love, and of a **sound mind**" (2 Timothy 1:7).* The person that sent out the word "crazy" has unknowingly drawn their sword against the person in which they are speaking to. At the same time, they have come against the WORD of GOD for that person's life.

In our society, the real definition of a word is now being ignored, and each generation has a fad of cursing one another. Television and mass communications have opened the door for a new way of speaking, and many souls have embraced it. This is because human beings are pack creatures, and we simply do not want to stand out. We learn to speak like the very crowd that we wish to entertain or be a part of. In addition, we try to avoid being labeled "strange" so we utilize every available moment to be seen as "cool."

As human beings, we easily pick up habits of cursing, and we get so accustomed to being cursed that these words often slip by unnoticed. Believe it or not, what is spoken into your life will attempt to manifest itself in your life because man was made in the image of GOD; meaning, we don't just bear resemblance to HIM, but we have HIS characteristics. When GOD said, "Let there be light," we know that light instantly manifested. This same life-giving power is in our tongues, but the enemy will use whomever he can to get them to speak death instead. There is power in our tongues, and we will have whatever we say.

There is absolute power in every word that you speak. This is why GOD commanded that we be changed by the renewing of our minds. We speak from the abundance or fullness of our hearts. In other words, we speak what we believe, and whatever we believe is what we have allowed into us or accepted into our spirit. To remove our demonic belief systems, we must first get back to the WORD of GOD. There are layers and layers of lies that are within each person, and each layer uncovers a new lie hidden under another layer. This is why it is so hard to come against certain beliefs that are in a man's heart. Your words are seed bearing words and will produce whatever you speak.

Word Curses

One of the issues that isn't talked a whole lot about is word curses, and how they affect our lives. That's because people often misunderstand the scriptures and many people who are religious are tuned in to hear what the Pastor is saying, but they refuse to hear what GOD is saying. That's not to say that GOD does not speak through your Pastor; it is to say that too many people depend on the Pastor, and don't have a personal relationship with GOD. Therefore, people come to church to grade the Pastor on his sermon based on how well he articulated his words, and how many scriptures he quoted that they already knew. The whole time, the Pastor is trying to get the people to lean on the LORD, they are leaning on the Pastor. So, they miss it all. They miss the WORD of GOD that flows from the man or woman of GOD'S mouth because they didn't come to the building to hear the

WORD; they came to be emotionally charged up, entertained and sent back home. People go to church and take in knowledge, only to leave it at the front door of their hearts, refusing to let it in.

But just what are word curses and how do they affect your life? Word curses are curses that were set in motion by our tongues. GOD made us in HIS image, and as such, we have the ability to produce or destroy. Because we are emotional creatures, we often use our tongues to do both; it depends on how our days are going. One day, we are speaking life and celebrating, and another day, we are speaking death and complaining. And because we have life-giving capabilities, what we speak takes form and lives. *"Death and life are in the power of the tongue: and they that love it shall eat the fruit thereof. " (Proverbs 18:31).*

When we are angry with others, we tend to speak curses over them; nevertheless, the average believer does not know or understand that they are speaking word curses. That's because many believers believe that to curse someone is to chant evil over that person while stirring a big black pot full of porridge and summoning up a spell. We've watched far too many scary movies, but the real thriller happens in our own lives and starts within our own mouths. The real spells are not always cast by women wearing black dresses, pointy hats and a memorable mole on their elongated noses! No. Real witches are men and women who look like you and I. People who have not yet learned to control their tongues, or filter what they allow into their hearts; therefore, they speak evil when the evil in them has been awakened.

People often speak of you and others what they want to see manifested in your life or in the lives of others, and this is done for various reasons. Nevertheless, you can't get caught up in the "whys" of being disliked because while you are asking questions, their words do come forward to wage war against you. That's why you need to actively cancel evil words spoken into your life, and the lives of your family every day of your life. Oftentimes, it isn't the professed enemy whose words you have to cancel. Many times, it is the ones you love and tell the most to who will speak evil words against an unsuspecting you because you are not like them, or because they want company in their misery, but you keep living in victory. In most cases, one of the most important lessons we all have had to learn was to just be quiet about what GOD is doing in our lives, and to reposition the people we allow into our lives.

What happens when someone attempts to speak a word curse against you, or when you speak evil against someone else? As mentioned earlier, those words take life because we have life-giving capabilities much like our FATHER GOD. We often like to chant that we are covered by the Blood of JESUS, and we are; but what is not understood is that we give GOD permission to bless and protect us when we stay in HIS will. NEVERTHELESS, when we go outside of HIS will, we are in the enemy's territory, and as such, we are giving him permission to speak into our lives. You can't go into the enemy's territory and then start rebuking him. That's like going into a strip club, and then calling 911 because the women there are naked. We are guilty by association. That's why GOD warned us in 1 Corinthians 15:33 this way: "Be not deceived: evil communications corrupt good manners." This scripture OFTEN goes ignored as we try to cultivate new relationships with people who are like us because many of us don't understand that we are not called to stay the same way tomorrow as we are today. We are going to change, but guess what happens when you go into transition? Those people who you were once like become offended because you left them behind in your decision to bloom. Because they are unsaved or immature, they do whatever they can to keep you from going to the next level...including speaking word curses at you. As a result, you end up in unnecessary warfare, and you end up learning a lesson through experience that you could have simply learned through the WORD of GOD.

Then; of course, there are those familiar relationships that we have established with family members and long-time friends who have been there for us through thick and thin. What's amazing is how dedicated we often are to other people, and we are oftentimes more dedicated to people than we are to GOD. As you go forth in HIM, HE will often call you to make some pretty hard decisions, and those decisions include walking away from people who have been there for us through thick and thin. Why? Because sometimes, we went through thick and thin just because we were connected to those people! Other times, we were connected to them because we were going through something thick and think, and this is where they live. They live in misery, and love when they have visitors. When we can relate to others, we befriend them...not understanding that we won't always be able to relate to them. Miserable people are fun to be around until you mess up and smile, and that's when you are in danger.

But what happens when evil is spoken of us, or we speak evil of others? When you are a child of the Most High GOD, and you stay in HIS will, evil stays within its own territory. You are safe in HIM. Evil is patient because it has been here before mankind entered the earth; therefore, evil will wait. If you come out of submission to GOD and enter sin, whatever was spoken of you may just manifest. Oftentimes, the LORD will set forth limitations as to how much the enemy can test you.

Satan had to ask GOD'S permission to touch Job. GOD allowed him to attack everything around Job, but he could not touch Job's life. He was even able to afflict Job's flesh, but he could not touch Job's life. Why was that? Because Job was submitted to GOD. When Satan wanted to attack Peter, he went to the LORD and asked for permission to sift Peter. The Bible tells us in 1 Peter 5:8 that the enemy goes about seeking whom he can devour. *"Be sober, be vigilant; because your adversary the devil, as a roaring lion, walketh about, seeking whom he may devour."* This clearly tells us that he cannot devour everyone; therefore, he seeks whomever he can devour. He could not devour Job; he could not devour Peter, so he asked to at least tempt them.

What does the word "tempt" mean? Tempt means to

test. When we hear the words "tempt" or "temptation," we often think of a seductive woman; nevertheless, seduction is only a form of temptation. Another way to tempt a man is to provoke him to anger. Why does the enemy tempt us? To trap us in disobedience, and to come outside of the safety of GOD'S will. When the enemy wanted to test Job, he wanted to prove that he could make Job curse GOD. He asked to sift Peter like wheat. To sift is to violently shake a sieve so one can distinguish between what they want and what they don't want. For example, when you sift flour, you are trying to separate the fine flour from the lumps. When you sift gold, you are trying to remove the sand from the gold. The enemy wanted to prove that he could find some evil in Peter, and he does this same thing to you.

The Bible calls Satan the "Accuser of the Brethren" (See Revelations 12:10). This is because he is always going before the LORD trying to accuse GOD'S people of wrongdoing. Thank GOD for JESUS because CHRIST bore our guilt on the cross and took captivity captive! He enslaved the slave master, and we can now walk freely!

This is what the enemy does to you: He tempts you to deal with people that GOD told you not to deal with. He tempts you to sit in seats that GOD told you not to sit in. He tempts you to review situations that you should have handed to GOD long ago, and if he can get you to trip, he then goes back and makes accusations to GOD about you. He petitions for the right to attack you. We call his presence an "attack" when, in reality, it is pure unadulterated temptation, and it can be weighty. If he can get you in rebellion, and you stay there, he can then tempt you because you are now in his territory. NOW...the words that people have spoken against you can actually come against you because you are on enemy grounds without any armor! Where is your armor as a believer? Ephesians 6:11-20 reveals this truth: *"Wherefore take unto you the **whole armour** of God, that **ye may be able to withstand** in the **evil day**, and having done all, to stand. Stand therefore, having your **loins girt about with truth**, and having on the **breastplate of righteousness**; And your **feet shod** *__with the preparation of the gospel of peace__; Above all, taking the __shield of faith__, wherewith ye shall be able to quench all the fiery darts of the wicked. And take the __helmet of salvation__, and the __sword of the Spirit, which is the word of God__: Praying always with all prayer and supplication in the Spirit, and watching thereunto with all perseverance and supplication for all saints; And for me, that utterance may be given unto me, that I may open my mouth boldly, to make known the mystery of the gospel, For which I am an ambassador in bonds: that therein I may speak boldly, as I ought to speak."*

Just like a man or woman tries to seduce you out of your clothes and into fornication (or adultery), the enemy tries to seduce you out of the armor of GOD so that he can sin against you. He wants to attack you, pervert you, persecute you, accuse you, sift you and then kill you because he hates you. Therefore, it is imperative that you stay in the will of GOD, wearing the armor of GOD because the enemy is seeking whom he can destroy.

When you are angry, you will find yourself wanting to speak word curses. This is the flesh's reaction to being provoked. Satan stands by to review and record your reaction. He is like a private investigator; he wants to show the footage to GOD of you being unfaithful to GOD. The enemy waits on you to curse that man out who keeps on harassing you. The enemy wants you to take revenge against that woman who keeps on provoking you. It is the will of Satan that you do these things, but it is the will of GOD that you stay put and know that HE (JEHOVAH) is GOD. Satan is always trying to get you (the believer) to use your mouth to curse others...even unbelievers! Notice how someone may cut you off on the highway and then "flip you the bird." You haven't committed any traffic offenses against this person, but they are obviously unbelievers who are on a power trip. First, they scared you by honking their loud horn at you, and then they almost ran you off the road. After all this, they still had the nerves to stick out their middle finger at you when you blew your horn at them. Now, you're in your car with your flesh ministering to you. Your flesh says to chase him down and give him a piece of your mind....or more. Your flesh says to beat him down and then minister to him when he's in the hospital recovering. That's your flesh! But the enemy had a purpose for such a meeting. He already has that unbeliever, but he does not have you. So, the unbeliever's job was to tempt you to enter your flesh so that the enemy could launch an attack against you from there. That's why you'll find that on these days, the rest of the day doesn't go so well. Everyone steps on your feet one way or another. You find yourself telling people about the idiot on the highway and what you wanted to do to him, but you don't tell anyone how good GOD is and how GOD protected you. In that one moment, the enemy was able to steal your testimony and get you to glorify him instead of glorifying GOD. That's all a complaint is. A complaint is praising the enemy. It's the same as saying that everything the enemy set out to do to you has been done, rather than speaking the WORD of GOD over your life. You end up using that day to speak word curses over a spiritually dead man who more than likely already has word curses lined up to attack him. Your words just have to get in line.

What should you do when others speak evil of you? Pay attention to the words "of" and "over." Notice I didn't say that they spoke evil "over" you, but that spoke evil "of" you. Over implies that you are in submission to something, and that thing is in control of you. Our head rests above our bodies, because our heads are the controllers of our bodies. When we are in CHRIST, CHRIST is the head, and we are the body of CHRIST. Therefore, when we are in GOD'S will, we are headed up by CHRIST so no one can speak evil "over" us because the LORD will cast it down. In this, we are guarded by the breastplate of righteousness. So, people have to resort to speaking evil "of" you. This means that their words have absolutely no power because they are not in control of you. When you serve the Almighty GOD, the words spoken of you have to submit to the WORD that GOD has spoken in you, and those words have no power against HIM. So...what next? Those words have to return to the sender and declare them a liar. As such, liars are already judged by GOD, and that person invites the enemy into their homes to do to them what they wished was done to you.

But what if you are outside of the will of GOD? If JESUS CHRIST is LORD over your life, HE has to be head of your life. This means that you are to walk in total submission to HIM, but when you make sin your head, you hand sin the remote control to your life. Again, this is why the enemy will try to tempt you by provoking you to wrath, or seducing you into your flesh.

There are word curses that many speak of themselves, and allow others to speak of them because of their ignorance or rebellion. For example, one of the most popular terms for women to refer to one another as is "female dogs." *(That's the rated PG version of that word).* You will see women refer to their friends as "female dogs," and then they'll laugh about it as if those words have no power. Additionally, people often call their friends stupid, crazy, dumb, foolish, senseless and so on. Truthfully, when a friend calls you outside of your name or calls you anything that Satan would call you, they have an issue with you in their hearts. Luke 6:45 reads: *"A good man out of the good treasure of his heart bringeth forth that*

*which is good; and an evil man out of the evil treasure of his heart bringeth forth that which is evil: **for of the abundance of the heart his mouth speaketh**.*"
Whatever lives in a person's heart for you will manifest in their words, whether they dress them up as nice or send them out without the masks...whatever your friends say of you, they believe of you! Even if they simply don't know the real definition of a certain word, they have defined it a certain way, and they believe you meet the criteria of that word as defined by their definition of that word. That's why you'd better beware when you witness them speaking that same word over one or more of their enemies!

People call one another "stupid" or "crazy" as a way of saying that the person is "funny." Why was the word "funny" replaced with the words "stupid" and "crazy?" It's obvious; it is a wile of the enemy. Today's generation speaks more word curses against their own friends than they do against their enemies. Nowadays, it is safer to have an enemy who does not think about you everyday or call you everyday, than it is to have a friend who can't go a day without calling you and speaking a word curse against you. One thing about words is that they cannot and will not be redefined; therefore, when someone speaks a word against you, it does not lose its real definition. Whatever they spoke "of" you will try to find a way to get "over" you.

When we speak word curses of ourselves, we often say things like:
"This _____ is killing me!"
"I know I'm crazy!"
"These kids are going to run my blood pressure up!"
"I just died."
"The devil is attacking me!"
I know that last one may have confused you because people often believe that the devil is attacking them, but this is not always the case. Sometimes, we are just getting a spiritual spanking because of something we did or we continue to do. For example....let's say a man went out and carried on an illegal relationship with a woman (fornication). As a result of their uniting, the woman conceives a child. Could that man

say that the enemy was attacking him by allowing that woman to get pregnant? Of course not! He did what it took to create a child; he had sex! So, the baby is not the result of the enemy attacking; the baby is the result of two people coming together and uniting their bodies like a husband and wife does. As a result, conception took place as it was supposed to. Sometimes, we are just in the midst of consequence trying to fight off the devil when he's not even there. Review how David did when he was chastised again and again for his mistakes. David repented and asked GOD for mercy! But today's saints will update their Facebook statuses to read something like, "Please pray for me. The enemy is attacking, but we know GOD gets the victory." And the people pray amiss because they are praying against the devil instead of restoring their brother in meekness. In other words....tell him the truth, but don't be puffy and self-righteous with it.

We have to pay close attention to the words that exit our mouths and what we allow others to direct towards us. Sometimes, the easiest way to see a person's heart for us is to pay attention to the words that keep dropping from their lips of us. Word curses have no power over the believer, but when the believer leaves the safety of obedience to live in rebellion, they have chosen to reject CHRIST and submit to HIS enemy. As such, they invite the plagues of the world, and every curse of the unbeliever to themselves...including words that were spoken against them.

What should we do when someone speaks evil of us, or when we unintentionally speak it of ourselves and others? When someone else speaks evil of you, simply cancel their words. You don't always have to know what was spoken; simply cancel every evil word spoken against you and your family every day. It doesn't matter if that day is a good day for you, or a not so good day for you. Submit yourself to GOD by doing HIS will, and always speak what HE spoke of you over your life.

Finally, be careful who you give permission to be in your life. Some people that we allow in our lives end up under the judgment of GOD because they weren't mature enough to be in our lives; therefore, they did to you and me what they do to others. They gossiped; they ridiculed; they persecuted, and they spoke word curses! That's just what they do. They are unbelievers or immature believers, but GOD said to touch not HIS anointed ones, and do HIS Prophets no harm. Whenever you know someone is a gossiper, it is safer for you to distance yourself from them than it is to associate with them in hopes that you are safe from their gossiping tongues. In dealing with them, you are giving them inside access into your life, and as a result, they will do what they are good at doing: gossiping! Should you minister to them? Yes, if they want to be ministered to, but this does not mean that you should hang out with them or tell them what's going on in your personal life. It means that when they need sharpening, you are there to sharpen them. When they need correcting, you are there to restore them in meekness. When they need edifying, you are there to edify them. This means you limit your communications with them to strictly the things of GOD! Outside of that, there is no communication because it will easily lead to evil communication.

Canceled words have to return to the sender because they are still bearing life. When you canceled them, you didn't kill them; you simply stripped them of their power in relation to you and your family. But those words were dressed a certain way and released, so they have to be cast out if they are not cast down. As such, they will return to the sender and become the sender's new roommate.

Don't go around complaining about what others say about you if you are hanging out with them! That's like hanging out with a bank robber and then acting surprised when your wallet comes up missing. You knew he was a thief when you invited him into your life. Stop thinking that you are exempt from the sinful behaviors of people. When a man will sin against GOD, he will have no problem sinning against you. It's time to change our language and learn to speak blessings over ourselves and others, and through this book, we are going to learn how!

Habitual Cursing

The average person speaks more word curses throughout their day than they speak blessings. It is very easy to announce what we see as the obvious, than it is to speak life into what we do not see. The issue is that there is some place in which we want to arrive at and it always seems so far away. Most of us have plans for our lives, but there is something that we want that looks to be the peak of the mountain. Not just arriving in Heaven; of course, most men want to go to Heaven and spend eternity with GOD. But there is somewhere we want to arrive at in our natural forms, and each day is a day in the journey towards or away from that destination. Most of us are driven by our "mountain's peaks." Nevertheless, the place in which we want to arrive at often seems so very far away. For example, there are many people who want to be happily married, own a home and be financially stable. This is what many refer to as the "American dream." Once we arrive at our "American dreams," our mountains seem to start again from where we are. Now, we want to add on to our homes or buy a bigger and better home. Our desires to reach the top of our mountains are often what keeps us motivated to continue each day. The ability to dream and foresee ourselves living in a way that GOD has promised us gives us the fuel we need to go throughout each day. All the same, it goes without saying that as a believer, most of us are driven by our desire to please the LORD above all things.

But our journeys are often interrupted by the enemy. He very well knows that GOD says HE will give us the desires of our hearts, but Satan wants to discredit GOD and cause the believer to believe his lies instead of believing the WORD. Therefore, Satan has developed his own language that he introduces to the believer everyday through challenges, evil imaginations and people. One of the words he loves to throw around is "can't." The word "can't" can serve as a cursed word because it often goes against the will of GOD for you and me. GOD already told us what HIS will for us is.

1. *"**I can** do all things through Christ who strengthens me" (Philippians 4:13).*

2. *"For all the promises of God in him are yea, and in him Amen, unto the glory of God by us" (2 Corinthians 1:20).*

3. *"Delight thyself also in the LORD; and he shall give thee the desires of thine heart" (Psalms 37:4).*

4. *"But seek ye first the kingdom of God, and his righteousness; and all these things shall be added unto you" (Matthew 6:33).*

As you can see, GOD has already decided to give each believer the desires of his or her own hearts. Nevertheless, GOD'S WORD is like HIS mighty hands extended to us, but it takes faith to reach up and grab what GOD has already provisioned for us. That's why the enemy likes to attack our minds to get us to believe that we can't have what GOD has already provisioned for us. He tries to get us to believe that GOD was not being truthful with us. Needless to say, GOD cannot tell a lie. As a matter of truth, it is impossible for GOD to tell a lie; nevertheless, Satan is the father of all lies. So, what Satan does is tries to stop the believer from believing GOD'S report (the truth), and get them to believe his own report (the lies). He does this because he hates the believer and he desires the praise of man.

In your life, there will be plenty of challenges that confront you along the way towards your final destination. Why are these challenges allowed?

1. **Many believers have a perverse heart.** First and foremost, it's because our final destinations, or "mountain peaks" are often derived through perversity. To be perverse simply means to be turned away from GOD or to turn away from GOD'S will for your life. The average person develops these desires along their journeys in CHRIST, and they get off the path of CHRIST to follow after their desires. Nonetheless, most believers will make a u-turn and head to church because they have changed the image of GOD in their hearts. They are now convinced that all they have to

---

do is participate in roll call at a church by being present and performing to show that they are still believers. After they leave the church building, they continue their journeys towards what they want. How is this perversion? Remember Matthew 6:33, which reads, *"But seek ye first the kingdom of God, and his righteousness; and all these things shall be added unto you" (Matthew 6:33).* GOD wants to add all of our desires to us. Again, HE told us that HE and HE alone would give us the desires of our own hearts, but most people are trying to get it for themselves. Consequently, in walking this journey powered by self-ambition, the believer is no longer on the path of GOD; they are on the path of the enemy. As such, the enemy can and will devour them.

2. **Many believers are self-driven.** Another reason these challenges are allowed is to get us to understand that JEHOVAH alone is GOD. Most people are accustomed to being independent, to the point where they try to co-parent with GOD, when they are HIS children.

Because of this, GOD will allow us to trip over our own imperfections until we learn to stand on HIS WORD and just trust HIM.

3. **All believers are in need of some sort of deliverance.** Most believers think that because they have been delivered from the grips of Satan that they no longer need deliverance. The truth is we have to constantly be delivered from ourselves. Satan doesn't drive us because he can't drive us; therefore, he introduces fear and evil imaginations to us to cause us to walk off GOD'S path. He taunts and tempts us daily, and many deviate from the path of righteousness to follow their desires or retreat from their fears. All the same, when we become believers, we still have to submit ourselves to GOD and resist the devil. The average believer has submitted some parts of their hearts to GOD, but has stored away some parts of their heart because they still think they need to drive that part. GOD wants your whole heart; therefore, HE allows these challenges to cause us to fully submit to HIM and stop being

self-driven.

4. **Many believers still agree with sin.** The average believer is intimidated by holiness and holy people; therefore, they continue to walk the same path as the unbeliever. When rebuked, many will quote Matthew 7:1, *"Judge not, that ye be not judged."* Others will sing the rebellious man's national anthem. The lyrics goes like this: "GOD knows my heart." 4. The issue is that many believers don't want to present themselves a living sacrifice, holy and acceptable to GOD because it requires sacrifice! So, many find and submit to ministers who misquote scripture and give them the green light to continue on a sinner's path. In truth, whatever you allow around you; you allow in you. Whomever you communicate with often will either ruin your useful habits, or start some good ones. Many believers even allow their relatives to bring their girlfriends and boyfriends under their roofs to sleep with them; especially if they are visiting from a far away city or state. This is error because the believer

is not standing for what he or she believes in. In doing so, they are in agreement with the person they associate with. *"Can two walk together, except they are agreed?" (Amos 3:3).* When challenged or rebuked about their lifestyles, they will begin to sing their national anthem, "GOD knows my heart." Many will defend the sinner, but few will defend the One who bores our sins at the cross.

5. **To strengthen us for the journey and perfect our faith.** GOD knows that even when on the right path, we will be challenged, tried and tested by the enemy. Because of this, HE allows us to be tempted, but not above what we can withstand. 1 Corinthians 10:13 reads, *"There hath no temptation taken you but such as is common to man: but God is faithful, who will not suffer you to be tempted above that ye are able; but will with the temptation also make a way to escape, that ye may be able to bear it."* Temptation is Satan's way of sifting us because he wants to show GOD the sin that is in us. GOD allows temptation because HE

wants us to see the sin that is in us, so we can cast our burdens upon the LORD. All the same, GOD teaches us through our temptation to lean and depend on HIM.

Along this path of life that we travel, the word "can't" will often be on the u-turn signs that litter our paths. Because of this, many believers begin to speak curses over themselves, their families and their destinations. The average believer will settle into a life of well-enough rather than continue towards the life that GOD has promised them. Many will burn up Heaven's phone line complaining about not having enough manna in their wilderness; never continuing forth to understand that GOD has called them to a better place. As a result, many believers never go beyond their wildernesses because they continue to speak the language of the enemy, rather than speaking the language of the Kingdom.

The word "can't" should not be used unless you are speaking the WORD of GOD. Let's review five examples of dialogues commonly used, and how they can be changed to benefit the believer.

Daniel: Marsha, will you loan me $20 until payday?
Marsha: I can't. I don't have any money.
Proper Response: I am awaiting the arrival of my paycheck as well. My apologies.

Marsha: Daniel, what did the doctor say about your wife?
Daniel: She will never be able to walk again.
Proper Response: The doctors said she will never be able to walk again, but GOD said that she was healed according to Isaiah 53:5. I believe GOD!

Daniel: There is no way that you will be able to manage this office, run a household and volunteer with the ministry team. I'm sorry; you just can't do all of that.
Marsha: Well, it's worth a try.
Proper Response: I can do all things through CHRIST who strengthens me.

Marsha: Daniel, I can't do this anymore. My marriage

is crumbling before my eyes!

Daniel: I'll be praying for you.

Proper Response: Stop carrying that burden. Whatever you cannot do, GOD can do; therefore, can't should not be in the question. It's a matter of changing hands. I will be praying for you.

Remember, it's good to pray for someone, but it is also required that you sharpen your brother or sister in CHRIST.

There are other words and terms we speak out of habit that should not be a part of our vocabularies. For example, when someone says something extremely funny, many people say to that person, "You are killing me!" Many say to their loved ones, "I love you to death." Another phrase that is new amongst the youth is, "I just died" when hearing something funny. No doubt, this is the enemy's way of teaching us to speak death and not life. Instead of saying, for example, "You're killing me," it is better to say, "You're too funny." The problem with most people is they want to find expressive words that catch one another's attention. This is our way of speaking with an exclamation point because we can't write it out to show them the intensity of how we feel, so we use expressive terms that ultimately come back to bite us.

When you speak a word, it goes out to accomplish what you said. This is because we are created in the likeness of GOD. (See Genesis 1:27). Your words will either head north or south. They will either go up to Heaven and pull down GOD'S will for you, or they will turn into hell and pull up Satan's will for you. Ask yourself often which direction your statement just went in. Pay attention to your words so you'll know if they are Heaven-sent or hell-bound.

Remember to speak what GOD has spoken, and to cancel any other word spoken into your life that opposes what GOD has spoken. Many word curses are sent out to you as imaginations by the enemy. He speaks the word curse in the form of a suggestion, but it has no power until you speak it and agree with it. GOD told us in 2 Corinthians 10:5 what to do with the words and images that visit our imaginations. *"Casting down imaginations, and every high thing that exalteth itself against the knowledge of God, and bringing into captivity every thought to the obedience of Christ..."* Sometimes, this won't be easy to remember when worry has entered the picture. Of course, worry comes when you believe Satan's report as opposed to GOD'S report. Instead of addressing the doubt Satan has caused you to submit to, address Satan with the WORD of GOD. You must always have your SWORD drawn. Remind him that GOD did not give us a spirit of fear; but of power, and of love, and of a sound mind. Remind him that GOD'S promises are yea and Amen. Remind him that no weapon formed against you shall prosper. Do not speak what the enemy has spoken because he wants you to speak against what GOD has spoken. Instead, always be ready to address him with the WORD of GOD until he flees. He will often return to test you again and again, but what he is doing (unbeknownst to him) is helping you to remember scriptures as you speak them, and causing you to search the scriptures for answers. Therefore, he ends up becoming an unwitting professor.

Profanely Jealous

There are many situations in life that brings out the worst in us. Every man has different buttons, but there is one button that can be pushed that will set off just about every man. Of course, when I say "man," I mean both men and women since wo<u>man</u> includes the word "man." That button is called "jealousy." Even the most astute of characters will find their inner curse words when they have been set off by jealousy. Nevertheless, this chapter isn't about how to curb jealousy; it's about how to change how we respond to situations...even the most intense of them.

Whatever you have in you that is unlike GOD will often hide in your heart. Of course, if you are trying to live a life that is pleasing to GOD, you want to make sure your heart is pristine because we know that FATHER lives in our hearts. In the olden days, the Israelites would build these beautiful temples with walls of pure gold, and this still wasn't enough to attract GOD'S attention. After they would build these immaculate temples, the Priests had to come in and bless the place. The Priests would sacrifice bulls and goats for the people, and only the Priests (Levites) were allowed in the temple.

Nowadays, GOD has given us an amazing gift, and that gift is the HOLY SPIRIT. The WORD tells us that we are now the very temple of the HOLY SPIRIT. Take a moment to think about that. You are the actual temple of the HOLY SPIRIT! Nevertheless, most people are still so grafted into the old Mosaic law that they still honor the building and not the LORD HIMSELF.; therefore, people put on their Sunday's best before entering what many refer to as the "house of the LORD." When they go back home; however, they are cursing, fornicating, drinking, smoking and committing every manner of sin and iniquity possible. This means that people go into an empty building and put on a show, but when they are outside of that building, they desecrate their temples. On Sunday morning, they are back at it...asking for prayer to change their situations and stop all of the attacks that are coming against their families, finances and health. What's wrong with this picture? Do we not understand that GOD is jealous concerning us? Yet, we can be jealous of other folks and understand the intensity of hurt we feel when we witness someone whom we are married to, for example, carrying on inappropriately with another person, but we can't seem to grasp how the LORD feels. Therefore, people go around cursing one another out and acting crazy when their significant others are in the arms of another person, but most can never understand why their blessings are not evident. Would you bless your spouse if you saw him or her making out with someone else? What if they were making out in the house you share together, but when they went to a family gathering, they put on their "Sunday's best?" If you were like most human beings, you'd want to call them out, but GOD is merciful...even though HE is jealous over you.

The term often used is "insanely" jealous. This indicates that jealousy has taken someone into the depths of insanity, and they aren't acting their normal self. The truth is jealousy does not make us lose touch with who we are; jealousy causes that iniquity that has been hidden in our hearts to come lunging forward. It can't hide itself when the fire of jealousy's wrath is awakened. It's like sitting in a burning building; you would come running out of there if you smelled smoke or noticed the flames.

Everything that is hidden in your heart operates the same way. When provoked, some of what is in your heart will show itself. When provoked by jealousy, whatever is hidden in your heart will swing open your heart's doors and make itself known. This is why many are "profanely" jealous. Whatever profanity or profane thinking we have is often hidden in the most religious of hearts; but sometimes, we endure fiery trials because GOD wants us to see what is hidden within the depths of our hearts. After all, HE lives in our hearts, so it goes without saying that HE would like to live in a clean place. You can't have profane thinking thrown around, gossip in the doorway and complaints spilling over into your praise. So, the trials come and they are never fun to endure, but they are necessary. The trials are simply GOD with HIS broom, sweeping the sin from under the hidden places in our hearts. This is to say do not despise the day of great wrath, for it is a day that has come to show you what is in you; what GOD is seeing every day. Instead of talking about who provoked you to curse or to behave in an ungodly way, you should be thankful that you got a chance to see what was hidden within the depths of your heart. We ought to want to know what is living in us because it affects our very lives. More than that, it is affecting our relationship with the LORD, and THIS is where we need to draw the line. Instead of trying to draw the line between our spouses or insignificant others (non spouses) and whomever else we feel is auditioning for a role in their hearts, we should always be consumed with making sure our hearts are in right-standing with GOD. Jealousy on the outside should always remind us of jealousy that may be taking place on the inside, when GOD sees bad words contending with the WORD. We should be ashamed for the LORD to see words designed to bless sitting at the

81

front of our lips, but words designed to curse sitting at the center of our hearts.

Take the time out to examine your relationship with the FATHER. How did you react the last time you were at your angriest? What words came out of your mouth? What actions did you perform as a result of that trial? Whatever you witnessed that came out of you is what GOD is witnessing in you. Repent of the sin; renounce the sin, and cast your burden upon the LORD. *"Cast your burden upon the LORD, and he shall sustain you: he shall never permit the righteous to be moved" (Psalm 55:22).*

Please know that just as there are terrorists that live in the "great ole" United States of America, there are terrorists that live in the heart. They are just like the terrorists who live here in the States. They silently sit by and enjoy the freedoms of our country, but it always happens.... they suddenly spring forth to carry out a deadly mission. Those missions usually cost us hundreds or thousands of lives. Whatever evil you have in your heart is a terrorist as well; sitting by silently and enjoying the freedoms of residing in your heart. One day, it'll suddenly spring forth to carry out a deadly mission if it is not cast out. Don't let this happen. Get rid of all the terrorists in your heart by submitting your heart to CHRIST JESUS. It is then and only then that you can live in absolute peace of mind. It doesn't matter what goes on around you; it is what is in operation in you that will determine whether you live a loving and peaceful life or if you die after living a hateful and chaotic life.

The Heart's Bowels

"A good man out of the good treasure of his heart bringeth forth that which is good; and an evil man out of the evil treasure of his heart bringeth forth that which is evil: for of the abundance of the heart his mouth speaketh" (Luke 6:45).

The Bible refers to the substance in our hearts as a treasure. When our hearts are good, the treasure is good, but when our hearts are wicked, the treasure is wicked. Think of it this way: Every time you eat something, it enters your digestive system through your mouth, and it begins the process of digestion. If you eat right, exercise and drink plenty of water, it'll eventually be expelled as waste. Even though that steak smelled great before it entered the body, it won't smell good when it comes back out. That's because it mixes with the bacteria in our digestive systems, and is processed by acids that are in our stomachs, as well as enzymes.

People are the same way. We are like a digestive system. Whatever we say to one another through communications such as speaking, writing and singing, is often mixed up along the way. It gets mixed up with lies, opinions and theories. By the time it comes out, it stinks. Gossip tastes real good going in, but the end result is always crappy. This is the very reason that GOD told you to watch your communications, and guard your heart.

Whomever you allow to speak into your life has just instructed your life, and because of this, they have set some words in motion to accompany you along your journey. That's why when we enter abusive relationships, we are often hindered from reaching our full potential. It becomes difficult to hear the silent whisper of GOD when you have a loud "insignificant" other yelling in your ear all of the time. What a person continually speaks to us, eventually makes its way into our belief systems. The wrong people will power us up when we are doing what they expect of us, and they will drain us when we are doing the opposite of what is expected. This is why it is extremely important for you to guard your heart by making sure the wrong person does not have access to it.

At any given moment, you are being fed something. If what you are being fed is not right, it's wrong. All the same, whatever comes into you will have to eventually come out of you. Howbeit, whatever we allow into our hearts stays with us and is continually expelled from us over the course of our lives. GOD told us to cast down evil imaginations and every high thing that exalts itself against the knowledge of GOD because whatever we allow to enter our minds will eventually enter our hearts if it is not cast down. Any thing that is not cast down, must be cast out; therefore, it'll eventually become an issue of needing deliverance. Anything that makes its way into our heart will start to pour from our hearts; not just in our words, but into our very choices. This means that any and everything that enters you has the power to change you and change your life! What others pour into you, or what you allow to enter you is powerful enough to make your life a miserable one; or if their words are blessed by GOD, they have the power to make your life better. People who are surrounded by evil associations often don't realize how these people are affecting their lives. They don't understand nor do they recognize that many of the events that have taken place in their lives were the direct result of their associations. Think about it. There were some situations that you were once in that would never have happened had you not dealt with a certain person. All the same, some of the right associations have been used by GOD to set into motion a sequence of events that have blessed you and continues to bless you to this very day.

Your heart has its very own digestive system. When the truth enters your heart, it never stinks to a man who loves the LORD. To a man who loves his lies; however, the truth carries a stench. When lies enter your heart, they stink to everyone around you...including the man who loves those lies. He may embrace them as they come out of you, and he may even welcome you into his life to speak more lies, but this isn't because those lies aren't affecting his life; it is because he's used to the smell. Think about how some people are. They carry an awful stench on their person and in their homes; nevertheless, they can't seem to smell the stench, and they don't understand why you refuse to sit down when you visit them. People get used to living in funk-filled places!

When the wrong things have been spoken into us and received by us, they begin a process similar to digestion. We mix what we believe in our lives, and we live with whatever comes forth from that mixture. For example, let's say that you have an Uncle Peter, and Uncle Peter does not respect women. Uncle Peter tells you over and over again that your wife cannot be trusted because she is a woman, and she has beady eyes. He is passionate about the words he is speaking to you, and he is always adamant that you need to watch her.

One day, you find her cell phone on the bathroom sink vibrating. Why doesn't she have her ringer on; why does she have it on vibrate? These questions puzzle you, but what really hits you hard is you recognize the number that is calling her. It is that no good Aunt Rita of yours, and you didn't even know she was still in communication with your wife. After all, you know that your wife is not fond of Rita, nor is Rita fond of your wife. You peak around the corner and notice that she is still in the kitchen peeling potatoes, so she won't be leaving the kitchen for a while. You go through her text messages, and find that your wife and Aunt Rita have been exchanging phone calls and text messages for a while. The text messages seem encrypted; nothing really makes sense, but you notice that Renee (your wife) is supposed to visit Rita later on today. With your heart hurting and your mind spinning, you reason within yourself to keep quiet and just follow Renee. So, this was it? Uncle Peter obviously knew something and was hinting around to you because Aunt Rita is his wife! Suddenly, no good Uncle Peter is looking wise in your mind's eye. Later that day, your wife excuses herself and tells you that she is heading to the store, and she's going to make a stop by a family member's house along the way. She'll be back in thirty minutes to an hour. You nod your head, holding back the anger and the pain that you want to unleash on her. As she pulls from the driveway, you slip on your sandals, scramble to find your keys and out the door you go.

At the store, you watch from afar as she enters the building, and comes out twenty minutes later carrying a bag and pushing a cart full of new luggage. You follow her as she approaches your Uncle and Aunt's home, but she parks behind the house. You're ready to confront her, but you hold yourself even more to see what's about to happen. Like a psychopath, you park on the street behind Uncle Peter's house, hide in the bushes in the neighbor's yard, and you watch as Aunt Rita comes out the back door and receives the bag from your wife. They talk for about ten minutes, and then some man you don't recognize comes out of the back door and greets your wife. He goes to the car to retrieve the luggage, comes back and hugs your wife and they all go inside. Now, you can't contain yourself anymore. You're ready to set some things ablaze, so you climb the fence and muscle your way into the house as they are attempting to close the door. Of course, everyone is baffled, but that's not the worst part. After humiliating yourself, the family explains to you that Uncle Peter had been abusive towards Aunt Rita and Rita reached out to your wife for help. She asked your wife to stop by the store and buy her some new luggage. She had your wife to buy the mayonnaise to make everything look legitimate just in case Peter is home, but he is not. The guy who greeted your wife turns out to be Aunt Rita's brother, who is there to help her move out. Aunt Rita had instructed your wife to keep quiet about what was going on because Uncle Peter is biologically your uncle, and she feared that you may warn him in advance since you love him so dearly.

Many would argue that the wife was wrong to involve herself in such a sensitive matter without the knowledge of her husband, and you are right! But his reaction to the matter is a direct result of the seeds Uncle Peter had sown into his mind. When he did not guard his heart, he allowed a seed to be planted that could have destroyed his marriage had the events played out in a different way. Believe it or not, people die daily as the result of an evil seed being sown into someone's mind. Lies are contagious, and the people who host them in their hearts like to infectiously share them to contaminate others. *"Wisdom resteth in the heart of him that hath understanding: but that which is in the midst of fools is made known" (Proverbs 14:33).* It is easier for a man to share his misfortune with others, than it is for a man of great wealth to share his wealth. This isn't just in relation to money. A fool opens his mouth and spreads his foolery without fail, but a wise man often holds his peace. Even though he is rich in wisdom, he doesn't share it with the simple man because wisdom is too high for a fool. (See Proverbs 24:7).

It works the same way as bad food. Notice when you eat food that is past its expiration date, or food that is contaminated, it'll paste through your digestive system at alarming rates of speed. It'll cause violent spasms in your stomach and colon, and then you'll spend hours running to and from the bathroom until your body has expelled all of the food. People are the same way. When a simple man is full of ignorance and foolishness, he will keep running towards you and anyone that will listen to share the contents of his heart. If you resist his words, he oftentimes will become violent with his words, or some even become physically violent. That's because a simple man is wise in his own eyes, and he desires to build an audience and a platform for himself. When resisted, a simple man does simple things.

Even though many people don't dine with wisdom, they are always full of something, and when their heart's bowels are full of wasteful information, they need a toilet to sit on. This is where you come in. People will often see you as their toilet, and when they release into you, your life will begin to stink. The way you stop people from doing this is by not allowing them to speak wrongful things into your ear. If you want to know a quick way to get a simple man to leave you alone, here it is: start teaching him about the Kingdom of GOD every time he sees you. A simple man who wants the WORD will receive it, and your communication with him won't be evil. You will be witnessing, and this is great! But a simple man who does not want the WORD will get upset when he's not allowed to curse, gossip or complain in your ear. Because of this, he will go away from you and dodge you whenever he sees you. You won't have to hide in the grocery store anymore when you see, for example, Sister Freda, who likes to talk for hours about nothing. All you have to do is reach into your purse or your bag, and pull out your Bible. Start ministering to her and refuse to let her speak for no more than two minutes. Keep cutting her off and telling her how good the LORD is. After a while, Sister Freda will start dodging you and hiding behind clothing racks and apple stands hoping you don't see her.

If you want to reach GOD'S desired potential for your life, simply submit your life to GOD and fill up on wisdom, knowledge and understanding. Don't go one day without filling up. Your life is like a vehicle, and the more you fill it with wisdom, knowledge and understanding; the further you will go.

Reactive Cursing

When your heart is full of iniquity, you will often react to sudden scares and intensely emotional situations by cursing. Have you ever seen a sweet, meek woman who seemingly couldn't hurt a fly suddenly curse? I'm sure you have. When you were in high school, you probably thought it was funny to sneak up on her and scare her because she would react by cursing. Any other time, she speaks with such a sweet voice, and she even talks about church a lot. But anytime she is startled, she curses like a sailor. That's because this is an underlying issue in her that has not been dealt with. That's why it's called an iniquity. Sin is something we may do in the heat of the moment, but iniquity is whatever evil has become a part of our daily lives or habits. This evil can go undetected for a lifetime because the characters we see on the forefront bear no resemblance to the characters hiding behind the masks.

2 Timothy 1:7 reads, *"For God hath not given us the spirit of fear; but of power, and of love, and of a sound mind."* As you can see from the scripture, to have fear is to have an unsound mind. Think about it. A person who is fearful is worried about something, and has already determined what could happen to them; therefore, they are always on the defensive. A man full of fear can be more dangerous than a man who is fearless because fear can drive a man to lengths that go far beyond humane behavior. So, when you find yourself cursing after being startled or angered, chances are, there is an underlying issue that has to be dealt with before you can stop.

In order to find the issue, you must first get past your pride. Pride is like a body guard for fear and every thing evil. It stands at the forefront of the heart and denies the presence of evil within the heart. If you listen to your pride, you'll turn around and say what pride says.

To get past pride, you must first humble yourself before the LORD. Humbling yourself means to terminate pride's employment in your heart. What better way to humble yourself than a food fast? This is the time where you can go before the LORD and just deny yourself completely. Deny yourself the food you want; deny yourself the pleasures you want, and deny yourself...period! As the days wear on, you will find that every underlying issue is a covering for another underlying issue. GOD wants to get to the root of the issue, because oftentimes, what you see on the surface is just a covering for what is beneath the surface. For example, a man may have a perverse spirit attached to him. He frequents church, but his heart is far from GOD. He watches porn daily, and he is into all sorts of ungodly sexual behaviors. Going to church (hypocrisy) was his way to cover up his perversion. Screaming in church was his way to cover up his guilt. Lying was his way to cover up his ways. Bribes were given to cover up his secrets. He has a whole list of issues that are there to further cover the root issue of being perverse. This is to say that you must address the underlying issue before dealing with the surface issue.

How do you address what lies beneath? Again, try fasting and being totally open and honest with yourself and GOD. If you are still hurt about something someone did to you, tell them that you are still hurt and ask the LORD to heal you. If you have to write a letter to that person (and then ball it up), do so. First and foremost, you have to deal with whatever lies under the surface. What if your parents were abusive towards you? A lot of people deal with issues such as their dads abandoning them, and this led to them witnessing their mothers bring in man after man into their homes. Their mothers ended up putting those men before their children, and this caused a whole lot of hurt, anger and unforgiveness; it changed how they viewed the world. Nowadays, they see women as a whole as evil creatures, and they befriended wicked older men in their search for a father figure. In cases like this, the first thing that has to be addressed is the abandonment and the betrayal of the mother. When we were victims, we thought and acted as victims; but when we came to CHRIST, we were supposed to wear our "more than a conqueror through JESUS CHRIST" gear. A lot of people find themselves constantly feeling sorry for the child that they once were. They can still see that child crying and wishing for a hug, but we have to move past our hurts to get to our victories. We cannot be victims and overcomers at the same time. You are either a victim or an overcomer.

To overcome the issues of your past, you have to understand them. There is no way to understand the choices of another human being unless you are the person in question. You will find that many of the people who have hurt you in your life were also hurt at some point in their lives, and they never healed from those hurts. Sure, you may know better and you may make a different decision than they made based on how you were handled, but this doesn't mean that they think the way that you do. Some people have many deep-rooted issues that go far beyond what you can see or what you've heard them say. Oftentimes, people keep their pasts in the past, but it lives presently in their hearts. They'll try to drown it with alcohol, blow it up in smoke or constantly hurt others because they too are hurting. If you happened to be someone in their line of fire, you were just a victim of a cycle that the enemy set in motion to play repeatedly. You can be the one to end that cycle by choosing to use whatever happened to you to glorify GOD. It's easy to say what someone has done to us, but it is better to focus on what GOD has done for us. If you are alive to read this book, you were granted another day to forgive and live the healthy, happy and abundant life that CHRIST JESUS has afforded us.

Sure, you won't get to the root of the issue in one day, but you'll get there if you give that burden to JESUS. Ask HIM the questions you want to ask HIM, and then cast that burden upon HIM. *"Cast thy burden upon the LORD, and he shall sustain thee: he shall never suffer the righteous to be moved" (Psalm 55:22).* Be patient; don't be anxious. *"Do not be anxious about anything, but in every situation, by prayer and petition, with thanksgiving, present your requests to God" (Philippians 4:6 NIV).*

As those issues are addressed, you will find yourself in situations that may seem provoking, but these situations come to show you what GOD sees. As you get closer to the LORD, and those issues are pulled out root by root, you will find yourself rejoicing at how you reacted. Situations that once caused you to curse will only tickle you. Situations that once provoked you to "knuckle-up," will only provoke a praise out of you. You see; the enemy may come and try to bring you back into your old ways, but if you don't focus on the people; instead, you focus on the spirit behind the people, you'll know how to handle the situation. Initially, you may find yourself upset at them for "letting the devil use them," but as time passes, you will learn the art of repositioning. This means; you will learn how to reposition people in your life or reposition them right out of your life so you can continue to grow. After a while, your life won't be about you anymore. You will find yourself helping others and actually thanking GOD that you went through what you went through when you see the face of a child who is where you once were, and you can reach out to them and pull them out of it. That's when you'll better understand that you were strong enough to endure the hurts of your past so you can help someone who isn't strong enough to endure the hurts of their present.

Think about how a bomb reacts. It has several mechanisms in it designed to respond to an action. Most bombs have gun powder in them, or some type of explosive additive. When it hasn't been provoked, that bomb is dormant; but once fire or some type of force comes in contact with the explosive additives in that bomb, it'll react by exploding. As human beings, we do the same thing. Whatever is in us can be dormant until something or someone comes along with enough power to get a reaction out of us. This doesn't always mean that the person is evil enough to pull such a reaction out of us; it only means they know how to locate our triggers, or they have enough power in them to get a reaction out of us. This means that we have to deal with ourselves and remove that power from their hands, so we'll stop exploding when they are around. Anytime a person has enough power to compel you to act outside of your character, please recognize the importance of that person in your life....for that season! They are there to show you the content of your heart. There are some ways in you that the LORD is not pleased with. Instead of responding to them; respond to your reaction. Use this as an exercise to know when you're better off. Once they lose their power in your life, they'll likely go away on their own because you'll lose your purpose in their lives. Some people like to jump-start other people just to watch their power in action, but when they lose this power, some walk away while others become extremely dangerous; therefore, be sure to pray about what to do before taking the next step.

Oftentimes, we want to remove the people from our lives who keep pulling our strings; but while removing toxic people is good, letting GOD remove the power they have over us is better. You'll often notice that every time you get rid of one problematic person, another one will surface or resurface in your life. Pay attention to your history. You may find that you abandoned a poisonous friendship, only to have another poisonous friend suddenly come back into your life. While you are busy telling the "found-again" friend about the last problematic friend, they'll be taking notes as to what provokes you. After a while, they'll start stepping on your toes, but in different shoes. *When you decide to rid yourself of them, they'll likely be more difficult to get rid of because they don't want to become like the old friend. Again, the enemy will send people for the sole purpose of tripping you up, but sometimes GOD will allow them to come forward because you allowed them to come forward. HE will allow that situation to teach you to stand on HIS WORD and stop falling beneath your own understanding, loneliness, attempts to fit in or attempts to find yourself. You will never react better until you learn to act better. A reaction is simply a re-occurring action that we have allowed to live, dine and sleep with us. When it becomes a part of your thinking; it is a part of your heart, and as such; it is an iniquity. That's why GOD tells us not to let the sun set on our wrath. We must deal with the problems of that day in that day. "Be angry, and sin not: let not the sun go down upon your wrath: Neither give place to the devil" (Ephesians 4:26-27).*

As you can see from the posted scripture, by not

dealing with the problems of today in the presence of today, you are actually giving place to the devil. This means that you are allowing the enemy to move in and reside in your heart. Recall what Peter said to Ananias in Acts 5:3: *"But Peter said, Ananias, why hath Satan filled thine heart to lie to the Holy Ghost, and to keep back part of the price of the land?"* Ananias lied; that was his crime. How was lying considered to be Satan filling Ananias' heart? John 8:44 (NIV) reminds of of how CHRIST responded to the Jews who were testing HIM. *"You belong to your father, the devil, and you want to carry out your father's desires. He was a murderer from the beginning, **not holding to the truth, for there is no truth in him. When he lies, he speaks his native language, for he is a liar and the father of lies."***

Our native tongue should be to speak blessings because to bless is the nature of GOD. After JESUS was arrested, Peter followed HIM...but, he cursed to prove that he was not with JESUS. Peter was denying CHRIST by cursing! This works the same way with us. When we belong to the LORD, our words should reflect that. When one tries to prove to others that they are worldly, they curse to deny CHRIST. They may throw up a scripture, or mention GOD; but in cursing, they are denying CHRIST so they won't be found out. *"Whosoever therefore shall be ashamed of me and of my words in this adulterous and sinful generation; of him also shall the Son of man be ashamed, when he cometh in the glory of his Father with the holy angels" (Mark 8:38).* When we are ashamed of CHRIST, we will be ashamed of HIS words. That's why you will find that when you are around certain people, you won't mention the LORD because you know this is not their language. They speak sin; you speak righteousness, but you know how to speak sin...so you do it and deny CHRIST. Instead, you have to let others know that you are in CHRIST and HE is in you. It does not matter where they are spiritually, you should not deny where you are spiritually. The worst thing they can do is avoid you. A lot of times, people feel pressured to show their old friends that they haven't changed because they don't want their old friends to feel betrayed by them. Who cares what they think? If loving the

LORD is wrong in their minds; why would you try to make them think that you are in agreement with them? It is true that some people can consider harming you when they know that you are no longer in the world, but this is why you have to let the LORD distance you from them. Just be obedient, and the LORD will cause the enemy to flee from your life.

The more you let GOD in your heart, the more you will have let HIS WORD in your heart, for HE is HIS WORD. As HE begins to fill your heart, you will notice how your actions and your reactions change. Instead of cursing, you will learn to call upon the Name of JESUS and this is where you should want to be. You should be in a state where even when you are angry, you glorify the LORD, trust in the LORD and call upon HIS Name.

Exercising Restraint During Trying Times

You may be a WORD-filled Christian who loves and adores the LORD, but you will be tried from time to time....some of us more often than others because of the people we allow in our circles. As a Christian, you have watched your speech and kept it clean. You have stayed away from gossip, idle speech and all sorts of evil communications. You have dressed your words with sweet perfume and delivered them with a smile to the people who wanted to hear them. But that spouse or those children of yours did it again. They said something to you that brought out a word or an army of words that you didn't even know were there. Now, you're off somewhere repenting and trying to find out how such wicked words could come from you. You have reasoned within your heart that "they" made you do it, but the truth is...no one can make you curse; they simply knew the right buttons to push to bring it out of you.

Remember, out of the abundance of the heart, the mouth speaks. Sometimes, we have soldier words that only come out when the battle has gotten too hot for our nice words. These words weren't absent from our hearts; they were simply hidden in our hearts, and when beckoned, they came out with their swords drawn. We spend too much time trying to clean up the words that have spilled out of our mouths, when we should have been spending that time opening up our hearts so GOD can clean them out. After all, that's where the real issue lies.

What do you do during those trying times when you want to "set everyone straight," and then retreat back to your Christian words? Trying times come to show you what is in you and who is around you. Sometimes, we have the wrong people around us, and these people are what the WORD refers to as "evil communication." Evil communication isn't just the conversations we have; sometimes, it's the people in which we engage with. No matter what you say or do with them, they will always try to bring the worst out of you, or put the worst in you because it is entertaining to them. If you attempt to minister to them, they will oftentimes laugh it off and start to speak evil against the Bible or the LORD Himself. That is a clear indication that the person should not be in your circle. When someone reveals their identity to you, believe what they have shown you and retreat if it is evil, and they want no part of GOD. Of course, if you are married, you will have to address this issue in another way. With a spouse, it's not so easy because they have almost around the clock access to you, and you can't just walk away because they aren't right with GOD. With a spouse, you will have to win them with your chaste behavior, coupled with fear. (See 1 Peter 3:2). This is NOT easy when dealing with a spouse, but you shouldn't see this as an attack from the devil through your spouse. Instead, let it reveal itself as training for you from the LORD. HE wants you to see what is in you so you can come before HIM in repentance, and renounce that mess. Every time you think it's gone, the spouse will "step on your toes" one way or another, and you'll find yourself witnessing first-hand what is in you. If it isn't the WORD of GOD that comes forward, you should retreat and deal with what has just marched out of your mouth. The Bible tells us that the WORD of GOD is a sword. If there is anything else coming forth when you are tried by fire, you need to get more WORD in you so that your automatic response won't be to use profanity or speak curses against others.

The slogan for Capital One is: *What's in your wallet?* What's funny about us is that we are more concerned about what we have in our wallets, pocketbooks and purses than we have about what is in our hearts. It is not what you have in your bank account that makes you rich or poor, contrary to what the world says; it is what you have in your heart that makes you wealthy with wisdom or rich with ignorance. At the same time, you can be poor in relation to wisdom just as you can poor in relation to simpleness. It is better to be starved of foolishness and pride than to lack understanding. It is better to have an abundance of wisdom than it is to have an abundance of things with no wisdom. That's why so many millionaires live miserable lives, and they end up dying prematurely. They had the world, but they lost their souls. The worst place you could ever find yourself in (besides hell) would be in a place where you have everything, but you don't have GOD; a place where you have great wealth and no one around who truly loves you; a place where you have thousands of supporters, but not one true friend; a place where you have people surrounding you, only to find that they are vultures following you. They are stalking you like a vulture stalks an animal in the desert. Vultures follow their intended prey for miles and wait on it to die. Many times, they began to feast on that animal when it is at its weakest, and almost at the brink of death.

What you have in your heart will determine the type of people that surround you, and the situations that you find yourself living in. The people around you will determine the words in which you speak because everyone has his or her own personal language. In order to carry on relationships with the people around you, you have to learn to speak their language. Remember what happened at the tower of Babel.

GOD confused every man's language, and they went away from one another because they could not understand one another.

Even passive people have a voice and a language that they speak. When you don't like the words that the people around you are speaking, and when you don't like what comes out of you when you are around them, it's time to change your friends. You wouldn't just consciously go out and find new friends, however. The goal is to submit your heart to GOD to be renewed so that the old information that caused you to be attracted to the crowd you once frequented will be removed, and new information will replace the old. We attract people based on what is in us. If you find that your friends are oftentimes rough around the edges, it is because you are rough around the edges of your heart. People often think, for example, if they see a woman with a biker gang, and she's a passive school teacher, that she just fell in with the wrong crowd. This isn't true. She simply fell in with her own crowd, but she just didn't look the part because she had put on camouflage to have the life that she'd been living.

To exercise restraint during trying times, you must first remove trying people from around you. In relation to the ones you want around you such as spouse and children, you have to change the way they communicate with you and how you communicate with them. Sometimes, you have to reintroduce yourself to people as a changed creature and require that they treat you as such. At the same time, you have to learn how to respond and when to respond so that your loved ones will learn your language. When you don't answer words you don't want spoken, you force others to speak new words to you. In other words, they have to learn to speak the Kingdom language just to address you.

When the people around you try your patience, it is always better to pay attention to how you react, rather than how they respond to you. How you react will tell you a lot about what is in you, and why you are surrounded by the people you are surrounded by. Going back to that meek school teacher in a motorcycle gang, if you ever want to know what her character is like, try her patience. She'd probably curse you out worse than the men in that gang. She'd probably pull the trigger of a gun faster than the men in that gang. Some of the most wicked people hide behind some of the most passive personalities.

When you notice that your reaction is highly charged, consciously rescue yourself from the situation, and go and deal with what is in your heart. At that time, get a pen and paper and began to write down what you want to say. After you have written down what you want to say in your anger, and then follow that sentence with how you want to respond as a changed man or woman. After that, start practicing saying what GOD would have you say, and do this in the midst of your anger. What you are doing is having an argument with the things that are in your heart. You are battling the flesh with the spirit.

While everything is okay, it is better to make a list of the words that you usually say in your anger, and then make a list of the words that you want to replace those words with. You can do this on the same sheet of paper or printable document. A great way to do this is to create a table in a Word document, and place the words side by side. Below is an example.

What I Always Say	What I Should Say
You're stupid.	I love you anyway.
You're a waste of skin and teeth.	You have beautiful teeth.
Go to hell!	GOD bless you.

Don't change your cursed words to better-sounding cursed words. Oftentimes, people may change saying, for example, "Go to hell" with "May GOD have mercy on your soul!" Either way, you are still saying that the person is damned or should be damned. When someone makes you want to curse them, try blessing them instead. I know that in your anger, blessing someone is the last thing that you want to do, but it's not about you. That's what you have to remember. Anger takes us to a place of selfishness, and we begin to try to defend the man or woman that we are. Anger is the evidence of pride manifested, and we all should know that GOD resists the proud; therefore, don't come against anger, come against pride. Humble yourself and behave opposite of how you feel like behaving. When you want to curse, bless instead. When you are feeling evil, it's not that the person has angered you, it is only that the evil that lives within you has made itself known whenever your strength failed. When your strength fails, your strongholds will always come out of hiding. Anyone can be a good Christian during happy times, but how hot does the fire of a trial have to be before the evil in you comes to the forefront? Many of us don't even need a lot of heat; when we are angered, the contents of our wicked hearts start bursting at the seams trying to come to the forefront.

When we have been provoked, we will always default back to who we have become. This is what we need to work on, because who we are today is a direct reflection of what we have allowed into our hearts. Even the people around us are evidence of what we have in our hearts. Have you ever seen a nice Christian man who praises the LORD with all his might on Sunday, hanging with thugs? I'm sure you have. At church and around "church people," he's calm, collective and seemingly holy. Around his thug buddies, he is known as "church boy," but he can be as brazen as his worldly friends. Why is that? He is a secular man who goes to church; he is not a "church boy" who hangs with secular people. Church, for him, is oftentimes a ritualistic act that he's been taught to perform in, but his spiritual habitat is around people who have like spirits.

When you want to do better, you must allow better in you. *"Ye are of God, little children, and have overcome them: because greater is he that is in you, than he that is in the world" (1 John 4:4).* If CHRIST is in you, HE will always make HIMSELF known during trying times. If pride, rage, unforgiveness, perversions, blasphemies and any other wicked devices are in you, they will make themselves known during trying times. What is in you reflects what you have been fed by and who you have allowed to feed you. When you want a changed life, you must make some changes to your mind. You have to reorganize your heart, and throw away everything that is unlike GOD. The people in your life are like furniture: some pieces just don't match your new mind; therefore, you need to move them out of your life. When you learn to strategically remove people from your life, remove yourself from certain situations, and allow GOD in your ears daily; you will witness a change in your life that once seemed impossible to you. Ask GOD to clean you up, and from there, start simply obeying HIM. It is then and only then that you will have good coming from you when the worst is upon you because better will be in you.

A Forked Tongue

"And the LORD God said unto the serpent, Because thou hast done this, thou art cursed above all cattle, and above every beast of the field; upon thy belly shalt thou go, and dust shalt thou eat all the days of thy life...." (Genesis 3:14).

We all know who the serpent is. He is the enemy of GOD; Satan himself. *"And the great dragon was cast out, that old serpent, called the Devil, and Satan, which deceiveth the whole world: he was cast out into the earth, and his angels were cast out with him"* (Revelation 12:9). What does this tell us about the serpent; the beast itself? It's simple....It used to walk upright. All the same, we know that Satan used to be upright; he was an angel of GOD, but his envy of GOD got the best of him.

There are some characteristics of the actual serpent

that we refer to as a snake that we should be aware of, and they are as follows:

1. **Snakes have no limbs**, but only a few of them have traces of limbs. In casting the serpent on its belly, GOD was removing every trace of HIS likeness from it.

2. **Snakes were once thought to be cold-blooded.** A snake can change to whatever environment it is in; therefore, it's temperature changes from hot to cold....depending on where it is! Bi-believers do the same. *"So then because thou art lukewarm, and neither cold nor hot, I will spue thee out of my mouth"* *(Revelation 3:16).*

3. **Snakes shed their skin several times a year.** Snakes shed their skin to allow for continued growth. When someone allows Satan to enter their heart, they become like his skin. The enemy will use a person with the intent of destroying them. He can't kill a person, but sin can; therefore, Satan entices a man to sin. James 1:15 reads: *Then when lust hath conceived, it bringeth forth sin: and sin, when it*

is finished, bringeth forth death. Once the enemy has seduced the man into walking in the flesh, he will then use the man to grow his kingdom. He will get him to seduce others into sin, hurt others and to create children after himself; children whom he will abandon or mislead. Satan knows that hurt people hurt people; therefore, if he can use that man to cause pain to others, he believes he can enter the hearts of the people hurt by that man. In this, the enemy has grown his agenda by using one man to open up the hearts of several men. His aim is to enter their hearts. He will then shed the dead man and use the souls hurt by that man to hurt others, and the cycle continues.

4. **A snake will never stop shedding its skin**, but it sheds it less and less as it ages. A young snake sheds its skin a lot because it is growing, but an older snake sheds even less. You will notice that an evil man, as he grows older, will lose his power. He'll still be evil, but because he is aged, he can't do as much

damage as he used to. That's why the enemy loves to catch people in their youth, and use them until they have sinned their way into death's bed. He starts anew with the people he has used this man to hurt. He comes in as a young serpent, and he grows his agenda by using these people to hurt as many people as he can convince them to hurt. Satan then uses this man at the peak of his youth; the time that he comes in contact with the most people. As this young man grows older, he loses most of power; nevertheless, the enemy will still use him to grow his dark kingdom, but he'll use him on a smaller scale because his youthful radiance, exuberance and energy are all things of the past.

5. **Snakes often shed their skin by brushing up against something hard.** A snake sometimes needs help completing its shed. If it doesn't shed properly, it can become blind....and blindness for a snake leads to a quick death! The enemy loves a hard heart, because he can brush up against it and grow

his agenda. The Bible refers to a hard heart as your flesh; therefore, Satan uses your flesh to grow! *"A new heart also will I give you, and a new spirit will I put within you: and I will take away the stony heart out of your flesh, and I will give you an heart of flesh" (Ezekiel 26:36).*

6. **A snake devours its prey whole.** Snakes have no limbs to transfer food into their mouths, nor are they able to chop up their prey; therefore, a poisonous snake will bite its prey and paralyze or kill it before starting the process of devouring it. A non-poisonous snake will often kill its prey by strangling it. Satan does the same thing! The enemy can poison some people, while he strangles others. Fear is a poison that he likes to use because fear opposes faith and it paralyzes the people bound by it. *"For God hath not given us the spirit of fear; but of power, and of love, and of a sound mind" (2 Timothy 1:7).* When a person fears what can happen to them, Satan then waits on them to confess this fear or to reverence him by acknowledging the fear. In

their confession, the person is wholly guilty. *"And the tongue is a fire, a world of iniquity: so is the tongue among our members, that it defileth the whole body, and setteth on fire the course of nature; and it is set on fire of hell"* (James 3:6). When a person is saved; however, they are under the law of grace. In this, the enemy cannot poison them, so he elects to strangle them. Strangling is a long process that involves letting the prey breathe, and then tightening ones grip every time the prey breathes. After a while, the predator will have cut off its prey's ability to breathe. As the prey loses consciousness, it first loses its sight and may become confused. Satan knows that the wages of sin is death; therefore, he entices believers to sin against GOD. Every time the believer sins, the enemy tightens his grip around them. He begins to squeeze them until they feel too guilty to praise the LORD, too prideful to humble themselves and too blind and confused to realize what's happening.

7. **Snakes have forked tongues.** Their tongues

are used like a second set of eyes since their vision is very poor. Snakes also use their tongue to aid them in the smelling process. Many people think that snakes smell with their tongues, but this is not entirely true. Snakes use their tongues to transport smell particles to the sensory gland known by many as the Jacobson's organ. The organ itself is what does the smelling. It helps the snake to find prey, avoid predators and sense mates.

The forked tongue is what we are here to talk about. Consider the fact that a snake uses its tongue to detect prey. Satan does the same thing. *"Be sober, be vigilant; because your adversary the devil, as a roaring lion, walketh about, seeking whom he may devour" (1 Peter 5:8).* This scripture reminds us that the enemy cannot devour every one; therefore, he goes about seeking whom he may devour. How can this be done? Is there some sort of light that encapsulates us and warns him not to approach us? Do we have a scent that lets him know we belong to CHRIST?

Like a snake, the enemy tests his surroundings to see which direction he can go in. Anyone that is saved knows that the enemy does launch attacks against them; nevertheless, he is unable to devour them wholly, so he tries to strangle them. This is why he asked to sift Peter. To sift something takes time, and involves a process of placing the substance to be sifted into a sifter. After the substance is in the sifter, it is then shaken until all of the fine parts of the substance has made its way out of the sifter, but the lumps will remain. Galatians 5:9 reads, "*A little leaven leavens the whole lump.*" The leaven referred to here is sin; therefore, Satan asked to look for sin in Peter by taking him through a grueling process.

But what is the deal with that forked tongue? Again, besides using that tongue to sense prey, the enemy uses his tongue to speak. Why is his tongue forked? Satan's tongue is split down the middle to represent the separating of truth from lies. The enemy can and does tell the truth (sometimes), and then he follows the truth with a lie because he is the father of all lies. Such is the believer today. On one side of their mouths, they speak the truth, praise the LORD, testify and even encourage others. On the other side of their mouths, they lie, complain, gossip and slander others. This fork in the tongue of the believer indicates that he is more like Satan than the man who is wholly in sin because the man who is wholly in sin doesn't care about speaking the truth or helping others. He cares more about himself. A man who is in church, but uses his tongue to speak evil has taken on the very nature of Satan because he hasn't chosen whom he will serve. Instead, he plays church (just like Satan) and then he accuses his brethren to GOD (just like Satan). What did CHRIST say to the church of Laodicea? *"I know thy works, that thou art neither cold nor hot: I would thou wert cold or hot. So then because thou art lukewarm, and neither cold nor hot, I will spue thee out of my mouth"* (Revelation 3:15-16).

GOD does not like when we play church because we become wise in our own minds. A person who plays church often doesn't see the need to serve the LORD wholly because they think by coming to church, falling out in church and even joining the ministry team that they are in right-standing with GOD...or at least close enough to Heaven to sneak in. Proverbs 26:12 warns against this. *"Do you see a person wise in their own eyes? There is more hope for a fool than for them."* Why is there more hope for a fool than a person who is wise in their own eyes? A person in sin is just that....a person "in" sin. When they decide to come out of sin, they are making a transition from the hands of the enemy into the arms of GOD. A person in church who knows what the WORD says, but has not allowed the WORD to penetrate their hearts has a stony heart. They enjoy their sin, but even after hearing the WORD, they have rejected HIM altogether. Their sin has now become iniquity, and their lives bear the leaven that leavens the whole lump; meaning, they can contaminate a whole church, just as they are wholly contaminated. A little sin made them wholly guilty, just as a little sinner allowed to act out his sin amongst the people of GOD can cause everyone to trip and fall into sin. When Satan is allowed to brush up against their stony hearts in the midst of believers, he is able to grow his agenda and following amongst those believers.

Remember, the nature of Satan is to mix truth with lies and then pervert the people of GOD. Even though your intention may not be to pervert the people of GOD, any time you speak evil, you send forth words crafted by the enemy to seduce others into sin or failure. Even if you tell what some refer to as a "white lie," you are still sending a lie at a person full of truth. When they believe that lie, it gets into their hearts and contaminates their hearts. This is the very nature and way of Satan. He only needs one lie in the heart of a child of GOD to begin hardening their hearts. He impersonates an angel of GOD because everything he does is designed to bring glory to himself and condemn the people of GOD. So the enemy uses people to bring other people to him! *"But what I do, that I will do, that I may cut off occasion from them which desire occasion; that wherein they glory, they may be found even as we. For such are false apostles, deceitful workers, transforming themselves into the apostles of Christ. And no marvel; for Satan himself is transformed into an angel of light. Therefore it is no great thing if his ministers also be transformed as the ministers of righteousness; whose end shall be according to their works."*

The words of your mouth mirror the condition of your heart. Is your heart a stony one that the enemy rubs up against to shed his skin and grow? Does your tongue speak right things, or are you divided in your words and ways? Are you cursing, complaining and speaking evil with your tongue; the same tongue you use to bless GOD with? Blessings and curses cannot flow from the same source; therefore, you have one master, but you must determine who he is. If GOD is your Master, speak right things...even in hard times.

In this chapter, we had to go deeper to get a better understanding of the nature of the serpent and how we put on its very nature by speaking with a forked tongue. We all know that lying is a sin, complaining is a sin and gossiping is a sin; but until you know the very depths of the reason such idle talk is sin, you will continually return to it.

Satan is a predator, but you can make him your prey

by continuing to serve the LORD in all that you do. When the enemy comes to attack you, you should simply stay in the will of GOD and bless the Name of the LORD. While you are there, ask the LORD to give you all the wisdom, knowledge and understanding that is in the midst of that trial. In doing so, you are preying on the predator. Instead of him strangling you, you will strangle him, and sift him for all of the wisdom stored up in him. You see, the enemy is not stupid; he was once an angel in Heaven. You simply become the "rabbit with the gun." You are now the predator searching out the prey. You would be AMAZED at how much wisdom and the goodies that follow wisdom that is in the midst of your trials. Truthfully, if you only knew what was there, you would ask for more trials!

Speak blessings every day, even on your bad days. This is how you turn a bad day upside down and shake better days out of it.

Canceling Word Curses

Over the years, there have been a lot of things said about you. People have spoken evil of you for various reasons. A lot of the evil that was spoken of you happened during your transitional years. These were the years after you made a lot of mistakes, and maybe stepped on some toes. These were also the years where you truly gave yourself to CHRIST, and the people who knew the "dead" you didn't like the "new" you. People would rather you step on their toes or even fight with them than to change. People will often speak the most evil of you during your transitional years because, as we transition, we have to leave some people behind. Some of the people we leave behind didn't have active or positive relationships with us, but they didn't like the idea of us passing them. Some of them did have active and positive relationships with us, and they often fear losing us. Because of this, people will often change towards you and speak the evil of you that they want to see come upon you. For example, your best friend may be intimidated because you have just been accepted into a large university. Instead of being happy for you, she decides that she doesn't like your choice to further your education. She goes about to speak word curses against you, and she does this without your knowledge. She says to others that you will not graduate, and you'll probably flunk out the first year. Is this what she truly believes? No. It is what she hopes for because she fears any change that occurs may affect your relationship with her, or she fears that you may change towards her. Now, she's speaking word curses against you because she is self-centered and hoping that the two of you can move up together, or she can move up and you'll stay in the same place. This really happens, and it happens often in human relationships.

You have to be extremely guarded when you are anointed by GOD, favored by GOD and chosen by GOD to carry out an assignment in the earth realm. GOD has an enemy that works through anyone he can, and his name is Satan, of course. Believe it or not, the enemy will and often does work through "church folks" and people who appear to be holy. A lot of people trust the souls who frequent the church building, not understanding that someone can frequent a building and still not be saved or in right-standing with GOD. Even in leadership! There are countless stories of people being moved by GOD from under the leadership of a church leader, and the church leader took it personal. People often form personal relationships that are rooted in self, rather than expanding the Kingdom of GOD. Because of this, many people speak evil of the ones who are parting ways from them.

What should you do when someone speaks a word curse towards you? First, always remember this: You are not always aware when someone speaks against you unless GOD makes you aware of it. Sometimes, HE may stir our spirit so that we can know the people we have in our circles are "different" and not in a good way. Then again, there are the times where HE may keep quiet because HE wants us to learn how to discern and stop being led by our emotions into relationships, partnerships and under leaderships. Whether you are aware of what someone has spoken of you or not, you should always cancel every evil word spoken against you. You should do this daily without fail. When you get a feeling that something isn't right, you should begin canceling words and commanding the angels that GOD has assigned to you to oppose any opposition that has been sent out to oppose you. All the same, remember to cancel any evil you may have spoken against anyone else. Sometimes, we do this out of habit; but this doesn't change the fact that the word or words we released were accursed. For example, you may be talking to your friend over the phone and he suddenly says something to you that is hilarious. Out of habit, you call him crazy, and tell him that "something is wrong with him." In doing this, you have just spoken a curse at him and called judgment upon yourself. Would you like him to be crazy? Would you like something to be wrong with him?

Some people would call this super-spiritual because

they lack understanding, but it is better to guard yourself and your anointing, than it is to keep tripping over words sent out to harm you. As you tune more into the heart of GOD, you may hear HIM suddenly say to you to cancel words spoken against you. Again, remember that life and death are in the power of the tongue.

Simply say this, after talking to the FATHER:
"I cancel every evil word I have spoken, and I cancel every evil word spoken against me and my family in the name of CHRIST JESUS." You must always cancel words in the name of JESUS because words are spirit and can only be addressed as such.

That's it! There is no big ceremony that you have to engage in because death and life are in the power of the tongue. When you canceled those words, you destroyed their power against you and your family. Recall what David said of his enemies in Psalms 59:7-12:
"Behold, they belch out with their mouth: <u>swords are in their lips</u>: for who, say they, doth hear?

But thou, O LORD, shalt laugh at them; thou shalt have all the heathen in derision.

Because of his strength will I wait upon thee: for God is my defence.

The God of my mercy shall prevent me: God shall let me see my desire upon mine enemies.

Slay them not, lest my people forget: scatter them by thy power; and bring them down, O Lord our shield.

For the sin of their mouth and the words of their lips let them even be taken in their pride: and for cursing and lying which they speak."

David not only prayed against words spoken against him, but he was a man of war. He specifically requested that his enemies be punished. Should we do this? No. Remember when GOD asked Solomon what his desires were, he asked for wisdom. This pleased the LORD so much that HE gave HIM wisdom and riches. HE said in 2 Chronicles 1:11, *"And God said to Solomon, Because this was in thine heart, and thou hast not asked riches, wealth, or honour, **nor the life of thine enemies**, neither yet* *hast asked long life; but hast asked wisdom and knowledge for thyself, that thou mayest judge my people, over whom I have made thee king."* Solomon did not ask for revenge against his enemies, and he had plenty of them. His focus was not on his enemies; his focus was GOD and HIS people. Over the course of time, you will find that many people will label you as their enemy, and for no obvious reason. There will be many cases where you were simply minding your own business, and someone comes along and decides they simply don't like you because people often categorize other people rather than individualizing them. You may remind one man of another man who once got in his face at work about a misunderstanding on the job. Because of this, he may categorize you and judge you from there. Now, every time he sees you, he seems guarded and rude. When he leaves your presence, he may say to someone else that you're no good, and then go on to speak all manners of evil against you. Of course, his problem is unforgiveness, lack of knowledge, lack of understanding, lack of wisdom....just plain lack! This means he is a poor man when it comes to spiritual substance, but he is rich in ignorance and overflowing with evil.

Just remember to bless yourself every day by speaking blessings over yourself. There will be times that just by speaking blessings over yourself and canceling evil sent out against you, that you will have changed the entire line-up of events that were awaiting you in that day. All the same, when you notice your day isn't going so well, don't speak more evil into that day. Instead, cancel evil words and every demonic assignment sent out against you. After doing this, begin to praise the LORD. GOD dwells in our praise. When you praise HIM, you call HIS glory upon you, and every wall that the enemy had stationed around you will fall and the enemy will flee.

Speaking the Kingdom Language

The Kingdom of GOD is like a whole new country. Kingdom people speak a language that the world does not speak. Sure, we may all speak the same earthly language, but Kingdom people speak blessings whereas the world speaks curses.

In the natural, if you have ever visited a foreign country where you don't speak the language, you may find yourself fascinated with the way the people speak, but you won't understand them. What's amazing is the fact that even within these countries, people often have their own dialects which distinguish what area of that country they are from. In many countries in Africa, the people within those countries speak multiple languages and dialects. A person can walk up the road in many African countries, and not understand the people on the other end of the road. This is because many countries have divisions referred to as villages, and the people of those villages have their own dialects or languages.

The words that you speak are a part of your spiritual language. They not only bear witness to where you are, but they reveal where you're from and where you are heading. You may encounter a lot of people in your life that look like nice Christian people. You greet them, and just mention the weather to them just to stir up small talk. Let's say you are standing in line at the grocery store, and the line is rather long. You greet the woman standing in front of you because she keeps looking back at you smiling. You compliment her hair and mention the weather. She smiles and when she opens her mouth, you suddenly realize that she is nowhere near Christ-like. She begins to joke and unleash all manners of cursed words, talking about everything from the beautician who styled her hair to the way the weather *bleeped* it up. Initially, you thought she was a woman of GOD because she was friendly and just had "that look" that you associate with Kingdom people. She is not of the same mindset as you, so even though you

146

understand her dialect, you recognize that she is of the world.

If you have ever entered the world of dating, you would know that there are plenty of men and women who will impersonate a child of GOD just to enter a relationship with you or lower your guards. They will attempt to speak Kingdom, but they aren't Kingdom-minded or Kingdom-headed. If you don't listen with the ears of discernment, you won't recognize the fact that they have an accent. What is this accent? Worldly people tend to speak as the world, and they can't hide their worldliness very well. Some of the most manipulative ones can, but most cannot. Even if you don't recognize the fact that they are worldly initially, after a few conversations with them, you will know where they are from....even the ones that frequent church. Please know that everyone that frequents church isn't Kingdom-oriented, Kingdom-minded, or Kingdom-bound; therefore, it is very important for you to have a relationship with the FATHER and learn to speak Kingdom so you'll recognize the imposters. *"Many will say to me in that day, Lord, Lord, have we not prophesied in thy name? and in thy name have cast out devils? and in thy name done many wonderful works? And then will I profess unto them, I never knew you: depart from me, ye that work iniquity"* (Matthew 7:22-23).

Recall the story where Peter denied JESUS three times. *"Now Peter sat without in the palace: and a damsel came unto him, saying, Thou also wast with Jesus of Galilee. But he denied before them all, saying, I know not what thou sayest. And when he was gone out into the porch, another maid saw him, and said unto them that were there, This fellow was also with Jesus of Nazareth. And again he denied with an oath, I do not know the man. And after a while came unto him they that stood by, and said to Peter, Surely thou also art one of them; for thy speech bewrayeth thee. Then began he to curse and to swear, saying, I know not the man. And immediately the cock crew. And Peter remembered the word of Jesus, which said unto him, Before the cock crow, thou shalt deny me thrice. And he went out, and wept bitterly"* (Mark 26:69-75).

In this story, you will see that Peter denied JESUS, but his accent gave him away. To further prove that he didn't know JESUS, he began to curse because it was unfitting for a man of GOD to curse. Of course, he did this out of fear because he didn't want to be taken prisoner and crucified.

Church people often do this, but not Kingdom people. There is a difference. Understand that we are the church, but some people see the building as the church, and they honor more the building than the temple that they are. They are religious in their ways, but they are not Kingdom-minded. They are terrorists trying to learn to speak the Kingdom language by sitting amongst Kingdom-minded people. They are foreigners, and their accents (worldly speech and ways) often betrays them. When you see them out amongst their element, they are cursing and carrying on as if they'd never heard the name of JESUS, but if they spot their Pastor or someone they respect, they will suddenly try to change their choice of words. Then again, there are the ones who are Kingdom-minded, but they fear being ostracized by the world, so they speak worldly when they are amongst worldly people. They try to disguise their Kingdom accents out of fear, and they will often deny knowing JESUS directly or indirectly. *"For whosoever shall be ashamed of me and of my words, of him shall the Son of man be ashamed, when he shall come in his own glory, and in his Father's, and of the holy angels"* *(Luke 9:26).*

In order to see a change in your life, a change must first occur in your heart. To see a change in your heart, you must first introduce change to your mind and then believe it in your heart. You need faith because faith is the only power that can remove sinful thinking and its residue. To get faith, you must get the knowledge of the WORD of GOD and believe it in. It's one thing to know what the WORD says, but faith is a whole new dimension where you have believed the WORD and been labeled as a "believer." There are many theologians who know the words written in the Bible, but they don't believe them because they (the theologians) are full of several kinds of doctrines. They have studied the Bible and every religious document they can get their hands on, and because of this, they don't believe in GOD. They become educated and start to believe that they are "smarter" than traditional church people and their Pastors because they have read more books and studied the history behind each book. Even if they say they believe in GOD, their dialect betrays them because they will speak more about their education and what they know than what the Bible says. They will often try to discredit scriptures because they have read a lot of conflicting information, and they have believed that information into their hearts. This simply indicates that they have studied many books and taken in the understandings of many people. As such, they begin to speak and even sound like the authors of the books they have read.

You will also encounter religious leaders who speak Kingdom, but they are not for or of the Kingdom of GOD. Matthew 7:21-23 reads: *"Not every one that saith unto me, Lord, Lord, shall enter into the kingdom of heaven; but he that doeth the will of my Father which is in heaven. Many will say to me in that day, Lord, Lord, have we not prophesied in thy name? and in thy name have cast out devils? and in thy name done many wonderful works? And then will I profess unto them, I never knew you: depart from me, ye that work iniquity."* Many people go to their churches, and even allow these people to prophesy into their lives, but the LORD calls them workers of iniquity. The expression "workers of" indicates that they were unrepentant. This was the state that they were in when they lived in the earth and when they left the earth. Iniquity means to be perverse, and perverse means to operate opposite of how GOD designed one to operate. Perversity also means to be stubborn and unyielding. For example, the Pharisees and the Sadducees were workers of iniquity. They knew scripture; they knew the Mosaic law, but even in that, they were hypocrites.

How can we learn to speak Kingdom? The language of the Kingdom of GOD is called faith. *"So then faith cometh by hearing, and hearing by the word of God"* *(Romans 10:17).* The New Living Translation states it this way: *"So faith comes from hearing, that is, hearing the Good News about Christ."*

We must hear the WORD to know the WORD. We must believe the WORD to truly understand the WORD. Why would we need to believe it first before we can understand it? To believe means to give permission to something to enter your heart through agreement. You must first allow CHRIST to enter your heart before you will receive HIM. There are many theologians who understand scriptures, but they don't believe the WORD. As we enter into a relationship with GOD, HE then begins to make known to us the mystery of HIS WORD. That's why you can read a scripture a thousand times, and it just won't make sense to you until one day it jumps off the page at you. At that time, the LORD has revealed to you what that scripture really meant. All the same, we can learn to pronounce a foreign word, and go to that country and speak that word to the people of that land, and still not understand it. After what we have spoken has been interpreted to us, it will then have meaning to us, and we will know how to use that word properly.

If a man knows scriptures, but has no revelation; to him, the scriptures are no more than a bunch for strange words on a page. Even though he understands the words he is reading, he may not know the WORD because he hasn't believed upon HIM; therefore, he won't understand the words because he does not understand the WORD. He will recognize the words and know what they mean, but he won't recognize the WORD because he doesn't know HIM.

What language do you speak? To speak as a mouthpiece for the Kingdom, you need to first learn what the WORD says. You need to frequent your church building, and more than this, read your Bible like your life depended on it....because it does. You need to meditate on the WORD of GOD so that you can believe the WORD. What we meditate on, or think constantly about, eventually enters our hearts and becomes one with us. We often read the Bible very quickly, never understanding the meaning of each individual word. Psalms 119:9-16 states: *"Wherewithal shall a young man cleanse his way? **by***

taking heed thereto according to thy word.

With my whole heart have I sought thee: O let me not wander from thy commandments.

Thy word have I hid in mine heart, that I might not sin against thee.

Blessed art thou, O LORD: teach me thy statutes.

With my lips have I declared all the judgments of thy mouth.

I have rejoiced in the way of thy testimonies, as much as in all riches.

I will meditate *in thy precepts, and have respect unto thy ways.*

I will delight myself in thy statutes: ***I will not forget thy word."***

As you can see, David is praising the LORD by acknowledging that he has hidden the WORD of GOD in his heart, and he commits to further meditate on GOD'S WORD. In this, he states that he has hidden the WORD of GOD in his heart to prevent him from sinning against GOD. From this, we can understand that without the WORD in our hearts, we will constantly sin against GOD. You can't speak Kingdom and not live Kingdom. You have to take the WORD of GOD in before you can live in the benefits of it.

Here's something you can do to change what is in your heart. Oftentimes, people try to change their words without allowing GOD to change what's in their hearts, and this is an error. When this happens, the person continually defaults back to their sin. To change what is in your heart, try meditating on the WORD of GOD and speaking it aloud several times a day. For example, let's say you were learning Psalms 1:1 today, and you wanted to learn that scripture by heart. You could meditate on it and you can go about your day speaking that scripture randomly.

When using language-learning software, the program will often teach you a new sentence and have you to constantly write and speak that sentence. After you pass that level, it will randomly throw that sentence at you as you study other levels. This is to ensure that you truly understand the sentence, and that you don't forget it. Do this with the scriptures. Let's say you have given yourself one week to learn Psalms 1. Everyday you meditate on every scripture in Psalms 1 line by line. Next week, you are learning Psalms 2. As you learn Psalms 2, you need to reintroduce Psalms 1 to your learning to ensure you don't forget it. As you enter Psalms 3, you need to throw some random scriptures from Psalms 1 and 2 into your studies. Additionally, you should randomly add scriptures from Genesis on up to ensure you don't forget them. You will speak, believe and live according to what you know, and as you get to know the scriptures, you will get to know the WORD.

Create a program for yourself that you can work with. Create a document and just list every book and chapter of the Bible in it that you have meditated on. Every day, randomly pick one of what you should already know and quote it. See if you can quote it from memory. If you can, that means it is in your heart. Think about what we say when we don't know someone's phone number off the top of our heads.

We say that we don't know their phone numbers "by heart." This simply means we have not committed their phone numbers to memory. Your goal is to commit the scriptures to memory. If you have trouble committing a scripture to memory, write it on several pieces of paper and tape it up around your house. Every time you see it, quote it.

Finally, replace the words you have learned to speak with the right words. Instead of calling your friends "crazy," call them "funny." Instead of calling your children "stupid," call them by their names. Instead of allowing yourself to be called anything that is not your name, correct the speaker in love, but with authority. Remember "hear a word, speak a word." If you speak the wrong words, cancel them out immediately. If you her the wrong words spoken, cancel them out immediately. You will find that the people whose time has expired in your life will get offended when you cancel the cursed words that they send out against you. After a while, they will disassociate from you. Why? James 4:7 says it best: *Submit yourselves therefore to God.* ***Resist the devil****, and* ***he will flee***

from you. It's simple. They were on demonic assignment!

Word Replacements

Replace This	With This
I can't...	GOD can...
Forget you...	I forgive you.
I give up...	I gave it to CHRIST.
You're stupid.	You're funny.
I don't know....	GOD knows...
You make me sick.	You make me pray.
I love you to death.	I love you to life.

Making Words Work For You

Imagine this: You hire a man to mow your lawn, and he does an okay job, but not a great one. Would you hire him again? Chances are; you would not unless he went back and corrected the issues you saw with your lawn. When you hire someone to work for you, you don't just want them to do an okay job, you want them to do an excellent job. That's understandable. Did you know that GOD has given you the ability to speak so that you could use your words to bless HIM, praise HIM and pray to HIM? When your words honor HIM, HE turns them around to honor you. Sin has perverted our hearts, and we now use words in the wrong way. They are now like that not-so-great lawn maintenance man; they work for you sometimes, and they work against you other times, but no matter how good or bad of a job they do, they still want to be paid.

But how can you make your words work for you? You

simply make it a point to become conscious about the words you speak. Fill your heart with positive words, and penalize yourself every time you use a negative word. Of course, you must first make your mind up that you want to see a change in your life, and you are willing to do this fast to set this change in motion. If you are unsure, you will likely step away from it when your heart has been challenged by someone else's actions or words. If you truly want to see a reversal in the direction of your circumstances, thinking and your life; this fast is perfect for you.

Before you start the word fast, you must first understand what words do to you, how they work for you and how they can work against you. In the earlier chapters, we discussed how words work against you, but let's examine how we can make words work for us. Remember, words have a job; therefore, they must be put to work.

Any time a word is spoken, it is given life. We are the mothers of words. The Father of the words we speak depends entirely on the words we speak. Satan is the father of all lies. (See John 8:44). JESUS is the Truth and the life. (See John 14:6). Therefore, we are always birthing life or death, depending on who we have allowed into our hearts. Of course, you can't birth curses and blessings because the two cannot flow from the same heart. Your heart is like a river, and a river cannot separate its waters. Whatever is in the river, is one with the water and will flow in the river and as the river. If you don't believe me, go and pour a cup of water in the river, and then try to gather only the water in which you poured into the river back into your glass. It's impossible. If you want to change what is in your heart, you must first stop damming up hatred, rage, unforgivenss and pride. These things must go from you so they won't flow from you.

To remove hatred, rage, unforgiveness and pride; you must deal with the root issues of each abomination. What has caused you to become hateful? What has caused you to become rageful? What happened to you that has caused you to enter unforgiveness? How did pride enter your heart? You must ask yourself these questions, and then answer the questions with the undiluted truth. If you dilute the truth in your heart, you won't get to the root of the issue. If you were molested, say you were molested and then confront the issue. You don't have to confront the molester; you can simply confront the issue. Tell yourself what the act has done to you, and then ask yourself what it has done for you. You can further confront an issue such as this by first forgiving the perpetrator, and then helping others who have also endured molestation to reach the river of forgiveness. Helping others will help you to see what happened to you in a more positive light. Of course, you won't be happy that it happened, but you can turn it around and help others.

If you have a wicked boss who keeps mistreating you, and you have found yourself wishing harm upon them, repent. To repent means to turn away from the sin and turn back to GOD. What you have to do is ask the LORD to place forgiveness in your heart for him, and then imagine yourself doing something good for him; imagine him coming to repentance. Imagine how happy GOD would be if this man was to give himself wholly to CHRIST. Then, make it a point to speak well to your boss in spite of how he speaks to you. Many people don't realize the power of love. It'll burn the heart of your enemies to see you loving them while they are hating you. At the same time, you cause them to enter judgment because GOD sees an opposing force coming against HIM....not you! When GOD is in you, whoever comes against you, comes against HIM. As such, HE will deal with them accordingly. This is why HE tells us that vengeance belongs to HIM. When we step outside of HIM, we come against HIM and place ourselves in the line of judgment.

But we need to put our words to work. Before they go to work, of course, we have to learn new words. A great way to learn new words is to simply open up your dictionary and memorize the positive words you find, and ignore the bad ones. Take the dictionary with you when you go to sit on the "porcelain throne." You can also Google positive words. For example, let's say you want to buy a new home, but the house you want is way past your budget. You are believing

GOD for this home, but doubt keeps arising. When doubt comes up, it simply means that you are lacking in faith. Lacking faith means you lack knowledge. Power up on your WORD! You can also study different words that demonstrate ownership and then begin to speak them in every sentence that leaves your mouth in relation to your new home. All the same, it is better to keep quiet about what you are attempting to do when your faith is lacking because the enemy will come against your words by bringing doubt upon you. Someone may walk up to you and ask you the latest news in relation to the home you want to purchase, and they may ask you if the loan has been approved yet. Now, if you have little faith, you'll end up speaking against what you have prayed for. You'll end up saying something like, "No. They haven't approved the house yet; I'm still waiting for their call." You have been praying and believing GOD that the house is already approved, but you just spoke opposite of what you prayed for. In other words, you sent out words of opposition to come against the very words you prayed and spoke previously.

Another good example is if someone was diagnosed with high blood pressure. They tell others about their diagnosis, pray against it and then believe GOD for healing. Someone approaches them and tells them that they need to put away the chicken sandwich that they are eating because "they have high blood pressure." Instead of canceling their words, the average person will continue to speak that they have high blood pressure, but that they can eat the sandwich. Remember, death and life are in the power of the tongue and those that love it will eat the fruit of it. The proper way to handle it is first, you shouldn't tell anyone if your faith is not where it should be. Secondly, if you have told someone; instead of saying you have high blood pressure, try saying that the doctor says you have high blood pressure, but according to the WORD in Isaiah 53:5, you are healed. Be sure to cancel the doctor's words. Please understand that many people have been healed from high blood pressure, cancer, diabetes and even HIV by simply believing GOD. What you believe, you will speak because it is of the abundance of your heart. Speak life to yourself, and speak death to high blood pressure.

As you learn positive life-giving words, challenge the people around you to speak life to you by speaking life to them. You can even start workplace contests where each associate who speaks blessings, and no cursed words for two weeks will be entered into a cup. Everyone who participates must give $10 to go towards this contest. If there is one person left standing at the end of the pay period, they get all the money. If there are several, you can either choose to place their names in a cup and pull a name for the money; or you can simply divide the money between all of them. After a while, this will become habit forming. Explain to them that the music they listen to will determine the language they speak so they need to change their channels if they really want to win.

Reward your good words by blessing yourself, and punish yourself for the bad words. Punishment can be simply fining yourself a total of $25 per bad word. You need to fine yourself an amount that stings. You can't fine yourself a dollar because there will be times where losing one dollar may seem worth it, but there won't be too many times where losing $25 will be worth it. Give this money to charity or a homeless person. You are tearing down a bad habit and creating a good one at the same time. You can even create a curse jar setup to be a blessing. Every time you curse, put money in that jar to go towards the charity of your choice. Be sure to call the jar a blessing jar instead of a curse jar. When you almost curse, penalize yourself. The aim is to remove the cursed words from your heart. Be sure to get rid of the money as often as you can to keep yourself from being tempted by it.

For every day you wake up, write down what you want in that day. What would you like to accomplish? What questions would you like answered? After you have done this, send up your prayer to Heaven and make your request known. Then, write down some "hunting" words. Their assignment is to bring back what you have prayed for. Of course, GOD will give it to you, but your arms of faith must reach out and grab them. The goal is to keep you from speaking against what you have prayed for. Let's say that you were praying for a raise on your job. What "hunting" words would you choose? Send the WORD after your promotion. *"For all the promises of God in him are yea, and in him Amen, unto the glory of God by us" (2 Corinthians 1:20).* Keep speaking that scripture over yourself. Also, speak the words: will have, can, mine, GOD said and amen. What you are doing is surrounding your blessing with positive words.

You can also use a tape recorder to record your positive words of the day, and play them continually throughout your day. Before you go to work, record them and play them. On your breaks, play those words. When you leave work, play those words. It may seem like a small thing to you, but what you are doing is making the life-giving capabilities of your tongue work for you and not against you.

Get everyone in your household involved as well. Tell your children that you will have to pay them $5 for every bad word you speak. They will keep you in check because they will learn to listen intently to what you are saying. Remember, cursed words aren't just profane words; cursed words are words that go against the WORD of GOD. Offer your spouse something they would want, but something that would feel penalizing to you. Again, don't say you'll take them out to eat if you curse because this may not seem like a punishment; especially on those days when you are hungry and want to spend time with the spouse. Instead, tell them that you'll take them on a shopping spree. Be sure to agree not to provoke one another to wrath just to penalize one another.

If you decided today that you want a brand new car; paid for in cash, you would have to work for it. If you went out and go a job, it may take a year or more to be able to save up enough money to go and buy a new car...cash. You have to put in a certain amount of hours, and you have to save a certain amount of money continuously. Believing GOD for what you want works the same way. Even when you decide you want something, you have to work towards it diligently. Don't give up because progress seems so far away. Decide to pursue progress so you can know at least that you are on your way towards it.

Use this concept with your words. Understand that even though you may send words out to bring something back to you, it may take a while before you see the manifestation of what you have been believing GOD for. That's because we operate in seasons, and there is a season for sowing and a season for reaping. When you are not reaping, you need to be sowing. Keep sowing good words, good deeds and blessings, and then the blessings of GOD will follow you. In order to be blessed, you must first be a blessing. GOD has created the things in life to attract after their own. Birds attract like birds; people attract people; dogs attract dogs, and cats are not attracted to lizards. In the same way, blessings are attracted to blessings and curses are attracted to accursed people. You have to learn to be what you want to have. Remember, what comes in our lives is there to bear witness to what we have allowed into our hearts or to try what is in our hearts.

Try yourself out. Pick up your phone and call your

friend and pay close attention to your conversation with that friend. Jot down the bad things you are accustomed to saying, and then jot down what you should have said. In addition, pay attention to what your friend is saying. Whatever dialect they speak, you understand because you are from the same place. All the same, you will be required to move when you learn a new language. Encourage your friend to come out of that place, if it is a bad place. If they refuse to move, please understand that you have to move on without them. That's what growth looks like! Sometimes, even in the natural, we outgrow certain people. You may have been a party-hopping, pill-popping druggie at one point in your life, but once you decided that you wanted better, you went for better. You also had to disassociate from those old friends who accompanied you in your self-destructive lifestyle because you knew if you didn't, you would return to the drugs and the partying. Getting further into the heart of GOD works exactly the same way! There will be people who you truly love and want to take with you, but you have to keep moving when they decide they don't want to go any further. Of course, you should minister to them and try to get them to continue in the journey, but if they are adamant about staying where they are, you have to leave them behind. You should never have more loyalty to a person than you have to GOD. You have to enter into HIS perfect will and not delay your arrival trying to entertain a relationship that was probably set up by Satan to be a stronghold.

Make your words work for you...literally. Consider yourself a patient in recovery. The WORD is your Doctor, and your words are your nurses. Be careful that you don't speak life into the wrong kinds of nurses; otherwise, your words won't nurse you to recovery; they'll mistreat you and abuse you until you stop calling them.

Word Fasting

Have you ever tried to diet before without learning why certain foods were good for you and why certain foods were not good for you? If you have, chances are you didn't lose any weight, or you didn't lose much weight. If you did lose weight, chances are you gained the weight right back. The reason for this is we are creatures of curiosity, and whenever we don't understand why certain things are not good for us; we'll often return to them. We'll reason within our own minds as to why we were told those things or people weren't good for us, and then we'll create a reason that they are good for us. Then we'll return to them, only to leave for good when we finally believe and have accepted that they are not good for us. This is the reason we discussed the power of words and how to change your words before talking about the actual fast. You need to know what the words are doing to you, and why you need to change the words that are in your heart. Think about having a daughter and telling her that she can't see her boyfriend anymore. When she asks your reason for prohibiting her from seeing him, you reply, "Because I said so." She will likely continue that relationship behind your back because she does not understand your reason for attempting to divide her from him. To get a better response, you would need to give her the knowledge that you have so she can better understand why you are against the relationship. Even though she may still go behind your back to continue in the relationship, she is more likely to end it when she starts realizing that you were telling the truth than if she never knew your reason.

We have to understand how our relationships with words are affecting our lives before we actually decide to break up with those words. If we don't understand, we will continue to have relationships with bad words and give birth to all manners of evil as a result of those relationships.

The word fast challenge is simple. You are to restrain

yourself from speaking certain words for a period of seven days initially. For example, don't say words like "can't" and "won't" because they are negative words. The only time you can use words like "can't" and "won't" is when you are referring to the enemy and what he can't do to you, and what he won't do to you. Other than that, stay away from those words. Be sure to inform your family and get permission from your spouse to start the fast if you are married. Why do you need permission? When the spouse is involved, they are more likely to respect what you are doing than if you just told them what you were doing. Some spouses may find it humorous to provoke you to curse while fasting, and this is why you need to discuss the fast with them first and ask them if they will honor what you are doing. If they'll do the word fast with you, that would be awesome. If not, don't worry; just continue if you've gotten their blessings.

Before starting the word fast, jot down words that you speak habitually. Pay close attention to your communications, and write down every negative word you find flowing from your mouth. Choose another word to oppose that word. You can find a list of words by Googling the antonym of the word you wish to oppose. For example, if you often refer to someone as "dumb," of course, you could start referring to them as smart. But what if "smart" doesn't feel right flowing from your lips? You can look up the antonym of "dumb" or the synonym of "smart." Your goal is to create a list of the words that you often speak, and then come against them. Also, you need to learn scriptures that oppose what you say. This will start to bring about conviction every time you say something that opposes what GOD says. Let's say you are married and you often say to your spouse, "You can't do anything right." Of course, you spoke a word curse at them. You can replace this statement with, "You can do all things through CHRIST who strengthens you. Try doing what you are doing through CHRIST." What you are saying is encouraging the spouse and speaking against any word curses that are presently active in your spouse's life. You'd be amazed at how the tide in your marriage could change if you just changed your words.

During the fast, you must commit to ending all evil communications. Those gossiping, profanity speaking friends of yours should be forbidden from contacting you that week. Eventually, they need to be forbidden from contacting you altogether. Be sure to commit to CHRIST to speak right things with HIS help for a pre-determined period of time. Don't let any profane or cursed words leave your mouth, and definitely don't allow any profane or cursed words enter your ears. You will have to limit yourself to certain movies and shows to keep from relapsing.

Here are a few tips to help you during the fast:

- **Don't do this just for you; do the fast for GOD.** Remember, only what you do for GOD will last.
- **Use the off button!** Stay away from people, music and television shows that promote profanity and cursing.
- **Don't answer the phone!** If one of your profane friends call, send them to voice mail. If your friends know that you have committed this time to fasting, and you have asked them to

not call you for that period of time, they should respect your wishes. If they call anyway, chances are, they are doing it to cause you to slip up or out of insecurity. Either way, don't answer the phone.

- **Utilize your peep holes!** Any time you are dealing with worldly friends, they will not honor the things of GOD. They will often test you to see if you are serious about your walk with HIM and if your relationship with HIM is more important to you than your relationship with them. You will likely get a knock at the door from a friend who doesn't understand why you won't answer your phone and why you are "acting strange." They'll likely give you some cockamamie story about having gone through some heart-wrenching incident to make you feel guilty. After this, they'll go on to question you about your distance. They may even try to provoke you. This is why you have to distance yourself for a week or so, and refuse to break your fast for their insecurities.

- **Just bless the LORD at all times!** Any time

you think to do so, speak blessings to the LORD. HE loves to be praised because HE truly is good and deserving of all our praise.

- **Speak blessings over yourself.** GOD doesn't mind when you speak blessings over yourself. In fact, this lets HIM know you have HIS heart. Just keep telling you how blessed, healed, beautiful, protected and rich you are.

- **Cancel curses spoken against you.** Never ever think that everyone likes you. In life, you will run into people at the supermarket who will dislike you for no apparent reason. This is why you need to get active in canceling all evil spoken against you.

- **Stay away from debt in every form.** Believe it or not, debt collectors speak curses over the people they are attempting to collect a debt from. At the same time, don't borrow from your friends, family or strangers. Be careful who you ask to help you with anything. There are a lot of people who will do something for you seemingly, but their hearts aren't for you. What they do for you is really being done for themselves, and they'll place a yoke around your neck as a result. Proverbs 23:7-8 talks about eating from the table of a wicked ruler. *"For as he thinketh in his heart, so is he: Eat and drink, saith he to thee; but his heart is not with thee. The morsel which thou hast eaten shalt thou vomit up, and lose thy sweet words."*

- **Reward yourself!** Reward yourself for going an entire day without speaking evil.

- **Punish yourself!** Penalize yourself from every wrong word that comes out of your mouth. Make sure the penalty hurts; otherwise, you will keep relapsing.

- **Give yourself to fasting and prayer.** You can commit to a food fast while on this fast...or not. It's up to you, but you must commit yourself to prayer.

- **Create your own unique/ positive slogans.** Sometimes we say the wrong things because they sound funny or witty. You can break this by creating replacement slogans or comebacks.

- **Mark the calendar!** Mark the calendar of the

days that you commit to word fasting. This way, once you are free from cursed words, you'll be able to tell people how long you've been curse-free. At the same time, seeing it marked on the calendar, will help to keep you committed to the goal.

- **Quarantine yourself.** There will be days when you have been provoked. Instead of coming against the provoker, excuse yourself to your room or to another area and give yourself to prayer. You need to be quarantined because your heart's infection wants to boil over. Don't infect the people around you; excuse yourself and glorify GOD.

- **Post about it!** Facebook and Twitter can be great places to tell your friends, family and complete strangers that you are committing to the challenge. Warn profane posters that they will be deleted if they use profanity. Better yet, if you have a friend's list full of profane souls, it is better to avoid those social networks altogether. If you want to visit the site anyway, don't read your feed when entering the site. Go directly to your personal page and begin posting from there.

- **Get others involved!** Most people love to have accountability partners, and to participate in something so positive. All the same, it will help everyone involved to stay committed to the fast.

- **Blog about it.** Tell others what you are going to do, and let them know you will be blogging about the experience. It'll help to get more people involved.

- **Verbally bless three people a day...at least!** Call, email or inbox blessed words to at least three people a day during the fast. Be sure to bless people who are GOD-fearing. *"Woe unto them that call evil good, and good evil; that put darkness for light, and light for darkness; that put bitter for sweet, and sweet for bitter!"* *(Isaiah 5:20).*

- **Turn the tables on the enemy!** When you are tempted to curse or speak profanity; rebuke the enemy and bless GOD instead.

- **Don't beat yourself up!** If you mess up,

penalize yourself or add another day to the fast. Rome wasn't built in a day!

- **Don't give up!** It may seem challenging at first, but you can do it. After a while, it'll be like lifting napkins.

- **See yourself in the impossible.** We know that all things are possible through CHRIST which strengthens us, but many people see certain lifestyles as impossible for them. Because of this, they get comfortable speaking in accordance with the lifestyle they feel they are trapped in or the lifestyle they feel is more fitted for them. Don't do this. Don't put GOD in a box. Envision yourself in that lifestyle, and believe GOD for it. Speak according to where you are going; not where you are or where you have been.

Any time you get the chance, commit yourself to this fast. Increase the amount of time that you participate in the fast each time you do it. Even continue the fast after your speech has cleared up drastically. Some times old ways tip toe back in word by word, and before we know it, we've reconciled with our old ways. The goal is to take it from being a fast to making it a lifestyle. This is why you are to increase the time in the fast each time you do it.

If seven days is too hard for you to start at; start with three days. Seven days are good to start with, but every man has his own pace and own faith. Some people are more extreme than others; while others are more stubborn than their counterparts. Keep turning up the heat and challenging yourself more and more. You have to get control of your flesh, and let GOD restore you back to your original design and purpose. We get perverted along the way in life, and we have to get back to who we truly are to start our real journeys of faith. It takes faith to get us there, and it takes faith to keep us there.

Do not give man what he expects of you. Who you were and who you are cannot merge, or your old identity will kill your new identity and take on his identity. Your old friends are friends of who you were, and in most cases, they will not welcome who you are now. You have to be willing to walk away from anything and anyone who attempts to place you in or return you to bondage. Many of us have established identities amongst our friends, and these identities were characters that we created to obtain and maintain our relationships. We became the life of the parties; the spark that started the fire, and the diamonds in the rough. When people who are familiar with the old us come in contact with the new us, they don't come to see change; they come to be entertained because again, we lived as their entertainment for far too long. Once they meet the real you, they'll likely criticize him and try to find a way to unearth the character that you were. You have to get away from anyone that anchors you in sin; there's simply no way around it. If you don't, you will return to your old ways and your friends will have their entertainment back. If someone does not want, appreciate or love who you really are; relieve them of having to deal with you, and relieve yourself of having to deal with them. You will find that every time you walk away from a friendship that has been holding you down, you will elevate to a whole new level of wisdom, knowledge and understanding. Every time you let go of someone that has been tripping you up, you will learn to stand on GOD'S WORD. Years down the road, if you stay in CHRIST, you will often find your old friends in the same place (mentally, spiritually, financially and socially) that they were when you last saw them. You; however, will be in a better place. It is then that you will realize just how far gone you once were and why it was necessary to abandon those friendships. You may not realize why you need to walk away now, but as GOD gives you more wisdom, knowledge and understanding....trust and believe, you **will** come to understand. This is called growth, and it witnesses to you that your life has continued to move forward in CHRIST. Think about your childhood friend from first grade. What if you ran into him today, and he was still in the same mindset? What if his mother suddenly handed him a coloring book and told him to go and sit down while he colored? You would undoubtedly ask the mother (or someone else) what happened to him because you will recognize that his development stopped at some point. At this, you will know that there is an underlying mental issue. Well, our associations (spiritually) work the same way. As you go forth in CHRIST, you will find that many people who you once loved to be around will be spiritually stunted at some point. When you come in contact with them again, they'll be in the same place they were in when you last saw them. In order to maintain those relationships, you would have to stay in the same place. This means that our relationships can and do stunt our growth!

If you have made up your mind to stop cursing, you have already taken the most important step in your life's change. Now, all you have to do is get the knowledge, apply it, preserve it and operate in it.

Please note that it takes on average 17-21 days to break a habit; therefore, you will have to conduct a word fast of 17-21 days before the habit loses its grip on you.

Word Feasting

We are all vessels, and we are always shipping around the contents of our hearts. We have to be emptied of all we are before GOD will begin to fill us with who HE is.

As you enter the word fast, you need to understand that you can't empty yourself of what is in you and stay on empty. When we evict words from our hearts, new words come to take the place of the old words. Let's say you decide to stop using the word "fool." You have learned to stay away from any and everyone who has earned that title, and when you come in contact with a simple-minded individual, you now refer to them as either "young in CHRIST" or "not born again." What you did was you replaced one word or line-up of words with a new word or line-up of words. Better than this, you have learned not to refer to them at all because you have ceased or limited your dealings with them. The problem with most broken relationships is that they were never supposed to be put together in the first place, or we gave people positions in our lives that they were not anointed to hold. Every position in your life requires the person in that position to possess a certain amount of wisdom, knowledge and understanding. When someone is given the position, but they don't have the proper tools to operate in that position, opposition will always ensue. That's because opposition is simply the opposing of a position. Think of it this way. What if you were married, and your marriage was in trouble? You go to your best friend who has never been married and ask for advice. In the beginning, she advises you to pray for your husband, humble yourself and give your husband time to bounce back from his not-so-humble hour. You pray for him, humble yourself and wait patiently for him to do the same, but he doesn't. Instead, he becomes more and more belligerent, and this is taking a toll on you. You go back to visit your friend, and you tell her the cruel things he's been saying and doing. She gets extremely upset and tells you to go home, pack your bags and move in with her until things cool off. This was an unwise move. Having never been married, she could not properly instruct you on what to do. She could give you some wise pointers here and there, but oftentimes, a woman is not married because GOD is still dressing her for her wedding. She may be dealing with some hurts from her past, and GOD is still removing those hurts before he puts HIS wisdom dazzled gown on her that HE'S designed for her. Because she's not ready, her love is not unconditional. Her love has limitations, and your husband has crossed her limitations by being so cruel. She will put herself in your position in her mind, and act accordingly.

Was she a bad friend for giving you bad advice? No. She was just not ready for the role you were trying to assign her to. You tried to add Marriage Counselor to her title, and she's unmarried and has never dealt with the trials that come upon married people. Therefore, you gave her a position, and if you take her advice, her words will oppose your position as a married woman.

What should you replace the words with? The WORD of GOD, of course. When you rid yourself of a particular word, learn a scripture in its place that relates to it. What you are doing is building a new habit. Remember, a habit takes 17-21 days to form or break. What you want to do is make a habit of speaking blessings daily, even when you're upset. So, for three weeks, you ought to make a menu of scriptures that you'd like to feast on daily. Read each scripture several times a day and meditate on each scripture. John 6:35 reads, *"And Jesus said unto them, I am the bread of life: he that cometh to me shall never hunger; and he that believeth on me shall never thirst."* The LORD is telling us that we do get hungry and thirsty, but not for food. GOD designed us a certain way, just as man designs a car. The car will hunger for fuel, and it won't move if the fuel tank is empty. As children of GOD, we hunger for wisdom, knowledge, understanding, faith and love. Every one of these builds upon another until you have reached the whole heart of GOD, for GOD is love. The LORD is telling us that with HIM, we will never hunger for wisdom; we will never be void of understanding; we will never perish for lack of knowledge; we will never thirst for faith, and HE will never leave nor forsake us, for GOD is love. HE is telling us that HE will fill every void in our lives; those very voids that we used fornication, drugs, alcohol, social media, relationships, food, television and video games to fill. This is the VERY reason you NEED to feast on the WORD! *"O taste and see that the LORD is good: blessed is the man that trusts in him" (Psalms 34:8).*

Feast on the WORD like never before, and don't go one day hungry. *"Wisdom hath builded her house, she hath hewn out her seven pillars: She hath killed her beasts; she hath mingled her wine; she hath also furnished her table. She hath sent forth her maidens: she crieth upon the highest places of the city, Whoso is simple, let him turn in hither: as for him that wanteth understanding, she saith to him, Come, eat of my bread, and drink of the wine which I have mingled. Forsake the foolish, and live; and go in the way of understanding" (Proverbs 9:1-6).*

Finally, please know that wisdom comes with a price.

Wisdom carries a rod of correction, and it'll begin to move things and people around in our lives, and this change (to us) isn't always welcome. As a matter of fact, it hurts; nevertheless, it is absolutely necessary. GOD repositions things and mindsets, removes and repositions people and purges our understanding to give us Truth. This process may sometimes feel a little overwhelming, but if you will see it through, you will come out of it glorifying GOD. Many people never reach their full potential because they retreat when the LORD starts to remove every trace of the devil from their lives. We've grown comfortable in our ways, mindsets and associations. It's can be very uncomfortable to have everything stripped away from you, people forbidden by GOD to continue with you and have no understanding to lean on for answers. That's why GOD has provided a Bible for you, and men and women after HIS own heart to encourage you along the way. Hebrews 10:25 states, "Not forsaking the assembling of ourselves together, as the manner of some is; but exhorting one another: and so much the more, as ye see the day approaching." To exhort means to encourage. As you go forth in the

LORD, your understanding will be opened by GOD in the right season. You won't have to search for understanding because understanding is in the hands of wisdom, and it is like a sweet dessert; once you taste it, you will be thankful for it.

"The rod and reproof give wisdom: but a child left to himself bringeth his mother to shame" (Proverbs 29:15). When we read this scripture, we often think it only means children under the age of 18. In truth, we are all children of GOD, and we start out in HIM as babes in CHRIST; therefore, we are corrected and reproved often because we are loved by GOD. HE knows that HIS people perish from lack of knowledge, so to save you, HE provides the knowledge for you through the coming together of the saints, reproof, correction and so on. Hebrews 12:6 reads, *"For whom the Lord loveth he chasteneth, and scourgeth every son whom he receiveth."* As we grow up in HIM, the correction may come less and less because we will know better, but when we are corrected, the rod may be bigger than that rod HE used when we were babes. Nevertheless, it is an honor to be

chastened by GOD because it is an amazing honor to be loved by GOD...especially since we don't deserve HIS love.

Throughout the good and bad times, as well as the word fast, you need to feast on the WORD of GOD. You need to be full of HIM so that when the enemy comes against you (and he will come), you can pour out of you what you have allowed GOD to pour into you. Every day, you have to prepare to stand your ground as a Christian, but you can't fight the devil with words; you can only fight him with the WORD of GOD.

Don't just fast and leave yourself empty. GOD wants to fill you up, but HE has given you the opportunity and the tools to open yourself up to HIM. Don't depend on man for your relationship with GOD. Your Pastor may be a GOD-filled, GOD-fearing and GOD-led man or woman of GOD, but their relationship with HIM won't get you into Heaven. It is your own personal and intimate relationship with HIM that will determine whether GOD says HE knows you or not.

Imagine that you are a man and a woman walks up to you and says she has three kids by you, and she wants to move her and her babies into your house. There is one problem; however. You have never seen this woman before, and if you have seen her before, you have never had any kind of sexual contact with her or even a personal relationship with her. She insists that you are the father and tries to find a way to move herself and her kids into your house. She tries to go to the court of law; she tries showing up on your doorstep, and she even tries breaking into your home. You would more than likely consider her deranged, right? So, when CHRIST says to a person, "Get away from me for I never knew you," HE is saying that HE did not have a relationship with them. They may have went around showing off their works and their words, and claiming they were a product of their relationship with HIM, but they were not being truthful. They were a product of that person's own self-worship, self-promotion and personal goals. In this, Satan would undoubtedly be the father of what they birthed out because Satan lords himself over selfishness and self-worship. For this very reason, we have to be serious about having a personal and intimate relationship with GOD. This means, we have to learn to seek HIM wholeheartedly; tell HIM our problems; ask HIM to deliver us from evil, and ask to be emptied of ourselves and filled by HIM. Many people will come before HIM thinking that their life reflected a relationship with HIM, when all it reflected was their knowledge "of" HIM, but no relationship "with" HIM.

Feast on the WORD, for HE is oh-so-good, and you will never thirst or hunger again. During the word fast, take the time out to denounce wicked words, renounce the enemy, pronounce the name of the JESUS and announce HIM as your LORD and Savior. The power to change your life is in your mouth!

Additionally, speak blessings over yourself every day. Say of yourself what GOD has already said of you. In saying what HE has said, and believing what HE has said, you are acknowledging that HE is LORD over your life; therefore, you are subject to every WORD HE has spoken over you. *"That if you shall confess with your mouth the Lord Jesus, and shall believe in*

*your heart that God has raised him from the dead,
you shall be saved" (Romans 10:9).*

There is power in your tongue, but don't use it in the wrong way. Use that power to bless the Name of the LORD, and HE will in return, bless you. That is to say, when you embrace HIM, HIS arms are already open to embrace you.

As you feast on the WORD, you will come in contact with trials that are designed by the enemy to bring you down, but the WORD in you will come forth to come against the enemy. Think of it this way. If a man walked up to you and started pronouncing all kinds of cursed words at you, would you turn around and start pronouncing cursed words at yourself? Would you agree with him and attack yourself verbally worse than he was attacking you? This is what happens when a trial comes upon us, and we begin to curse and act ungodly. The enemy tries to curse you by getting you to curse yourself. Instead of cursing, start blessing the Name of the LORD in the enemy's presence. Submit to what GOD has said over your life and not what Satan is saying of your life. Praise GOD harder than you have ever praised HIM. In doing this, you will shorten the length of your trial because the enemy will get up and run away from you. *"Submit yourselves therefore to God. Resist the devil, and he will flee from you" (James 4:7).* All the same, don't forget to ask the LORD to give you the wisdom in the situation. You'll get wisdom any and every time you endure and come out as more than a conqueror through CHRIST JESUS; therefore, be sure to ask for all of the wisdom in that situation. That's like having a good meal and licking the plate; you're refusing to let even a morsel go to waste. Sometimes, we overlook some wise points when we stare too hard at the points that stand out the most to us; nevertheless, every inch of wisdom is filling and should be taken in.

It's time to feast on the WORD of GOD! It's time to walk in a new day as a renewed you. Let your strength always be in the LORD, and HE will sustain and protect you in your going out and coming in. Pay attention to the words coming out of your mouth, and any time you see a terrorist word, come against it with the WORD of GOD. When you're challenged by a hardship in life, and those military words come marching forward, remember to pay attention to them to see which army they are from. If they are from the army of the LORD, they will bless the Name of the LORD. If they are from the enemy's army, they will curse everyone out and speak all manners of word curses because they were designed by the enemy to defile you. *"Not that which goeth into the mouth defileth a man; but that which cometh out of the mouth, this defileth a man" (Matthew 15:11).* Remember, GOD has HIS own army; if you are not marching with HIM, you are marching against HIM.

www.ingramcontent.com/pod-product-compliance
Lightning Source LLC
Chambersburg PA
CBHW060239050426
42448CB00009B/1509